CIVIL WAR LEADERSHIP AND MEXICAN WAR EXPERIENCE

CIVIL WAR LEADERSHIP

AND

MEXICAN WAR EXPERIENCE

KEVIN DOUGHERTY

UNIVERSITY PRESS OF MISSISSIPPI / JACKSON

www.upress.state.ms.us

The University Press of Mississippi is a member of the
Association of American University Presses.

First edition 2007

∞

Library of Congress Cataloging-in-Publication Data

Dougherty, Kevin.
Civil War leadership and Mexican War experience / Kevin Dougherty. — 1st ed.
p.   cm.
Includes bibliographical references and index.
ISBN-13: 978-1-57806-968-2 (cloth : alk. paper)
ISBN-10: 1-57806-968-8 (cloth : alk. paper) 1. Generals—United States—Biography. 2. Generals—
Confederate States of America—Biography. 3. Command of troops—Case studies. 4. Mexican War,
1846–1848—Influence. 5. United States. Army—Biography. 6. Confederate States of America. Army—
Biography. 7. United States—History—Civil War, 1861–1865—Biography. 8. United States—History—
Civil War, 1861–1865—Campaigns. I. Title.
E467.D688 2007
973.7′40922—dc22

2006100157

British Library Cataloging-in-Publication Data available

Contents

vii Preface

I Patterns of the Military Profession

PART ONE. THE FEDERALS

37 George McClellan and Siege Warfare

45 Ulysses S. Grant and Logistical Risk

51 Philip Kearny and Reckless Courage

56 Samuel Du Pont and the Naval Blockade

64 Winfield Scott and the Changing Nature of Warfare

69 John Pope and the Influence of Zachary Taylor

81 George Meade and Missed Opportunity

86 Jefferson Davis and the Bad Example

91 Joe Hooker and the Administrative Side

96 William Sherman and Room to Grow

100 Henry Halleck and the Military Executive

105 Henry Hunt and the Organization of Artillery

110 George Thomas and the Rock

PART TWO. THE CONFEDERATES

117 Robert E. Lee and Turning Movements Based on Reconnaissance

122 Pierre Gustave Toutant Beauregard and the Exception that Proves
     the Rule

127 Jefferson Davis and Misplaced Confidence

133 Braxton Bragg and Jefferson Davis

138 John Winder and Wartime Governance

143 John Slidell and Doomed Diplomacy

147 Gideon Pillow and Political Generals

154 Stonewall Jackson and the Role of Artillery

158 James Longstreet and the Changed Mind?

164 George Pickett and the Quest for Glory

169 John Pemberton and Inflexibility

174 A. P. Hill and the Tendency to Criticize

180 Lewis Armistead and Comrades Becoming Enemies

184 Summary of Lessons Learned

APPENDIXES

187 A. Federal Civil War Generals Who Also Served in the
     Mexican War

191 B. Confederate Civil War Generals Who Also Served in
     the Mexican War

195 Works Cited

203 Index

PREFACE

History is full of examples of how a soldier's experience in one war can impact on his or her conduct in another. Dwight Eisenhower attributes Winston Churchill's World War II penchant "always to see great and decisive possibilities in the Mediterranean, while the prospect of invasion across the English Channel left him cold," to "an inner compulsion to vindicate his strategical concepts of World War I, in which he had been the principal exponent of the Gallipoli campaign" (D. Eisenhower 194). For William Manchester, Douglas MacArthur's amphibious turning movement at Inchon in Korea came as no surprise because "[i]t had long been MacArthur's manner of doing things, as he had demonstrated along the New Guinea–Philippine axis, most notably at Hollandia" in World War II (372–373). John Taylor concludes that "the influence of the Korean War on [Maxwell] Taylor . . . went far beyond its immediate outcome. . . . Korea appeared to be a confirmation that the United States could confront Communist aggression virtually anywhere in the world and bring about at least an acceptable conclusion" (187). Taylor would carry this optimism into Vietnam (Taylor 321). Tom Clancy writes that "Vietnam was never far from [Fred Franks] throughout Desert Shield and Desert Storm" (18). For his part in Desert Storm, Norman Schwarzkopf considered it "crucial not to repeat the mistakes we'd made in Grenada" (343). Certainly there is much analysis yet to be written about the impact of Desert Storm on those who also served in Operation Iraqi Freedom.

Perhaps the richest example of this phenomenon is the impact of the Mexican War on those men who would go on to become the leaders of both the Federal and Confederate forces in the Civil War. In his aptly titled *Rehearsal for Conflict: The War with Mexico, 1846–1848*, Alfred Bill writes, "For the great conflict that was to come, [Mexico] was a singular preparation. Almost all of the officers who became famous in the armies of the Union and the Confederacy learned their grim trade in Mexico and gained some knowledge of the virtues and shortcomings of the American volunteer soldier, who was to make up the bulk of the armies they were to lead against each other" (ix–x). Herman Hattaway and Archer Jones echo this same thought writing that "the Mexican War was in a real sense a dress rehearsal for the Civil War leadership" (17). Russell Weigley asserts, "The biography of almost every officer destined for high command in the Civil War is ornamented with feats of skill and valor in the Mexican War" (*History* 185). The reach of the Mexican War experience into the Civil War is undeniably powerful.

In order to provide the proper context, this particular study begins with a discussion of the patterns of the military profession before both the Mexican War and the Civil War. But rather than viewing the influence of the Mexican War on the macro scale, the book proceeds to personalize the subject by depicting the unique experiences of twenty-six men in Mexico, thirteen who would later serve the Confederacy and thirteen who would remain with the Union, and tracing the Mexican War's influence on their conduct in the Civil War. General conclusions on the impact of service in Mexico are captured in the section titled Summary of Lessons Learned. Indeed, no other volume so exclusively and thoroughly focuses on biographical studies of the impact of service in both wars.

In many cases there is insufficient evidence to "prove" conclusively that a certain Civil War behavior was learned directly in Mexico. Indeed, some personality traits such as temperament may have been already formed in the soldier, and he thus acted in the Civil War as he acted in Mexico not because he learned something there but simply because that is the way he was. In other cases the man may have had strong experiences outside of Mexico, perhaps even early in the Civil War, that shaped his conduct as much or more than Mexico did. This book does not try to argue the exclusiveness of the influence of the Mexican War, merely its importance and its usefulness in understanding the Civil War. It uses the Mexican War experience to explain, predict, and illuminate Civil War behavior, tactics, and decisions. Admittedly, there are alternative explanations for certain Civil War behaviors than the Mexican War experience, and these are briefly noted in discussions of men like Braxton Bragg, John Pemberton, and George McClellan.

In some cases the influence of Mexico is speculative but certainly plausible, such as with George Meade, James Longstreet, and the Federal Jefferson Davis. Few Civil War commanders left testimonies that they acted in a particular way because of their Mexican War experience. The connections offered in this book "make sense." Granted that not all would necessarily "stand up in court," but even with this caveat, the conclusion is undeniable that the impact of the Mexican War was more rather than less.

On the Confederate side, there is Robert E. Lee, whose experience as a young engineer in Mexico taught him the value of reconnaissance and the importance of terrain in turning the enemy. There is Pierre Gustave Toutant Beauregard, who, unlike Lee, failed to learn this lesson and would maintain a stubborn preference for the frontal attack at Shiloh. There is the Confederate Jefferson Davis, whose experience in Mexico convinced him of his own military skill and led him to develop a very involved and direct approach to managing military affairs as president of the Confederate States of America. There is Braxton Bragg, who was with Davis at Buena Vista and, on the strength of that shared experience, maintained Davis's confidence longer than he should have. There is John Winder, who learned governing a defeated and occupied city in Mexico is different from governing a loyal population in Civil War Richmond. There is John Slidell, who would experience diplomatic failure in both wars. There is Gideon Pillow, who appears to have learned nothing himself from Mexico but serves as a notorious example to all of the dangers of political generals in both wars. There is Thomas (Stonewall) Jackson, whose devastating use of artillery in the attack in Mexico could not be readily repeated on the changed battlefield of the Civil War. There is James Longstreet, who marred perhaps by his frequent exposure to the high cost of offensive operations in Mexico would be decidedly partial to the defense in the Civil War. There is Longstreet's friend George Pickett, who would seek to relive the glory he so cherished from Chapultepec at Gettysburg and beyond. There is John Pemberton, who learned an inflexibility in Mexico that would not serve him well at Vicksburg. There is A. P. Hill, who was unsparing in his criticism of his fellow officers both as a lieutenant in Mexico and as a lieutenant general in the Civil War. Finally, there is Lewis Armistead, who represents the hundreds of soldiers who in the Civil War faced lifetime friends and comrades in arms from Mexico.

On the Federal side, there is George McClellan, who witnessed the success of Winfield Scott's siege at Vera Cruz and then unsuccessfully tried to emulate it at Yorktown. There is Ulysses S. Grant, whose service as a quartermaster under Scott taught him that an army could reduce its line of supply and survive, a tactic Grant repeated at Vicksburg. There is Philip Kearney, whose daring combativeness would cost him an arm in Mexico and his life in the Civil War. There is Samuel Du Pont, who performed blockade duty in Mexico and would then apply the lessons he learned there as president of the Navy Board during the Civil War. There is Winfield Scott, the undisputed genius of Mexico and model for so many junior officers, who would not be able to keep pace with change by the time of the Civil War. There is John Pope, who served in Mexico not under Scott but under Zachary Taylor and therefore received a different model that influenced his treatment of civilians in the Civil War. There is George Meade, who saw Taylor fail to finish the enemy at Monterey and then did the same himself at Gettysburg. There is the Federal Jefferson Davis, who as an enlisted man in Mexico would witness a case of violence and insubordination that would be eerily similar to an incident in which he would participate in the Civil War. There is Joe Hooker, who would serve on six different staffs in Mexico and use this experience to institute sweeping administrative reforms in the Army of the Potomac. There is William Sherman, who recognized the shortcomings of his limited experience in California and would give himself room to grow in the Civil War. There is Henry Halleck, who, like Sherman, saw almost no combat in California, but who translated the executive military management skills he learned there into useful administrative service in the Civil War. There is Henry Hunt, who would serve under the premier artillerist to survive the Mexican War and then apply what he learned as the chief of artillery for the Army of the Potomac. And there is George Thomas, who would learn a personal determination backed by strong artillery in Mexico that would serve him well as the "Rock of Chickamauga."

These officers provide a representative sample of the experiences of some of the men who served in both wars, and their Mexico experiences offer a small clue toward understanding the motivation and logic of their Civil War decisions and actions. The impact of these experiences is far-reaching, as evidenced by the listing in two appendixes of 194 Federal generals and 142 Confederate generals who served in Mexico. The appendixes have been compiled from a variety of sources, including *The Mexican War: A Compact History, 1846–1848* by Charles Dufour and *Generals in Gray and Generals in Blue* by Ezra Warner. Henry Adams said that "all experience is an arch, to build upon" (Bartlett 634). For these Civil War leaders, their arch was Mexico.

Civil War Leadership and Mexican War Experience

Patterns of the
Military Profession

Before beginning a discussion of the individuals who comprise this study, it may be useful to place their experiences in the context of the greater military environment before the Mexican War and before the Civil War. Current military doctrine lists the elements of combat power as maneuver, firepower, leadership, protection, and information (FM 3-0, 4-3). These elements provide a convenient means of grouping the lessons learned from Mexico and describing the military environment. The individuals selected for study in this book were chosen specifically for their ability to illustrate how these elements of combat power existed both in the Mexican War and the Civil War.

MANEUVER

Maneuver is "the employment of forces, through movement combined with fire or fire potential, to achieve a position of advantage with respect to the enemy to accomplish the mission" (FM 3-0, 4-4). McClellan's predilection for siege warfare, Du Pont's blockading ability, Lee's preference for the turning movement, Beauregard's preference for the frontal attack, Longstreet's tendency toward the defensive, and Pickett's love of the offensive are all examples of maneuver.

MANEUVER AND JOMINI

Both before and after the Mexican War, the United States looked to Europe for its instruction in the art of war. The most influential strategist of the

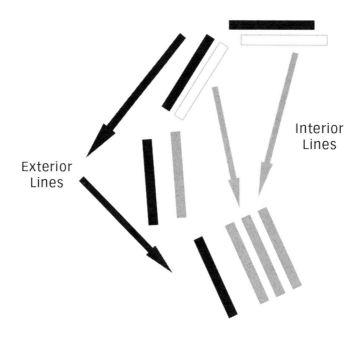

European military theorists was Antoine Henri, Baron de Jomini, who became the principal interpreter of Napoleonic strategy for the American military.

Jomini was intellectually rooted in the eighteenth-century Enlightenment. Thus he was offended by those elements of Napoleonic warfare he found chaotic and indiscriminate. In their place, he endeavored to use order and logic to define the principles of war in a way that formed a neatly organized system.

The result was an almost geometric approach to warfare. For Jomini, the problem was to bring the maximum possible force to bear against an inferior enemy force at the decisive point in the theater of operations. This condition could best be achieved by properly ordering one's lines of communication relative to the enemy's so that the friendly force possessed "interior lines." Interior lines allowed the friendly commander to move parts of his army more rapidly than could an enemy operating on exterior lines. In this way, the force operating on interior lines could defeat in detail an enemy operating on exterior lines (Weigley, *American Way* 81–83).

Jomini's influence would be felt both in the Mexican War and the Civil

War. Winfield Scott's focus on the geographic location of Mexico City rather than destruction of Antonio Lopez de Santa Anna's army is an example of the application of Jomini's concept of the decisive point in the Mexican War. Stonewall Jackson's Shenandoah Valley Campaign and Ulysses Grant's Vicksburg Campaign are examples of the use of Jomini's concept of interior lines in the Civil War. Indeed, Jomini's Civil War influence was so great that General J. D. Hittle asserted, "Many a Civil War general went into battle with a sword in one hand and Jomini's *Summary of the Art of War* in the other" (Donald 38).

MANEUVER AND TACTICS

At the same time the American army was learning strategic lessons from Europe, it also was modeling its tactics after European practices. Sometimes the predominant example was taken from the French, sometimes from the British. Always, however, American infantry were trained to attack in closely ordered linear formations behind a screen of skirmishers. Disciplined volleys of musket fire were the key to gaining an advantage, and the ultimate result would be decided by a bayonet assault (Donovan et al. 24).

In 1835, Scott's three-volume *Infantry Tactics* was adopted as the authority for infantry drill, a position that it maintained through the Mexican War and beyond. Scott's tactics emphasized disciplined order over speed, and mass over maneuver. He stressed close-ordered lines of either two or three ranks and discouraged the use of any movement faster than the quick-time rate of 110 steps per minute. Loose order was allowed only in skirmishing tactics where advanced troops deployed forward of their main lines to cover their own troops and to develop the enemy's fire. Each regiment would have one company of rifles or light infantry to act as skirmishers for the entire regiment. Indeed, such skirmishers would be a feature of the Mexican War, but they were only deployed in small numbers as a reaction to terrain and circumstances (Gabel, *Vicksburg* 36).

Scott's *Infantry Tactics* proved to be very appropriate for the situation in Mexico. In fact, its popularity was maintained by many units, mostly volunteers or state troops, in the early years of the Civil War. In the bigger picture, however, things were changing. The rifle and the minié ball necessitated a change in tactics, and in 1855 the army adopted Major William J. Hardee's *Rifle and Light Infantry Tactics* as its standard. In spite of the manual's promising title, Hardee's modifications were rather modest. Aside from increasing Scott's rate of advance to a double quick-time speed of 165 steps per minute, most of Hardee's changes affected instruction of how to handle the new weapon rather than battlefield tactics. The latter changes were destined to be immense, but would have to wait before they would be fully realized. For the time being, military men expected that the new developments would simply modify the existing tactical environment, not completely overthrow it. They were wrong (Weigley, *History* 190; Gabel, *Vicksburg* 36; Doughty 96).

Only limited efforts were made after the Mexican War to keep abreast of unfolding military developments. For example, when three officers, including George McClellan, were sent to Europe to observe and study the Crimean War, they prepared a lengthy report in which they devoted much discussion to the leggings used by Russian soldiers but failed to say anything about the much more relevant Russian conscription system (Doughty 97). Even more significant, the report made no mention of the use of the rifled musket and the dramatic impact this development would have on future warfare. Stephen Sears concludes, "As a consequence, neither [McClellan] nor those who read his report were stimulated to rethink tactical doctrine as a result of the Crimean War" (*McClellan* 49).

In an effort to provide some reform, Secretary of War Jefferson Davis had prescribed light infantry tactics for all units. This meant reducing the line of the infantry from three to two ranks and placing increased emphasis on skirmishers. Nonetheless, formations remained rigidly in the old Napoleonic style, with men standing shoulder to shoulder and intervals between units small. A brigade in this tight alignment would occupy a front of just 1,300 yards, and a division attacking in the common "column of brigades" occupied a front of similar length. The lines were maintained rigidly parallel to allow for a massed or uniform volley at the halt and to maximize the shock effect. Commanders knew such a formation presented a vulnerable target, but they believed that an attack coming in successive waves would eventually overwhelm the defenders and carry the field (Matloff 182; Williams, *History* 193).

What was left for Civil War commanders to discover was that the greater accuracy of the rifle would force men in these shoulder-to-shoulder battle lines to increase their dispersion and lengthen their lines. As individuals spread apart, the density of soldiers on the battlefield decreased. The increased ranges also led armies to form for battle farther apart. This increased the distance over which an infantryman had to advance to close with the enemy. The dangers of this prolonged exposure to enemy fire greatly strengthened the power of the defense, and battles came to be decided much more by firepower than shock action. All told, battles took longer to fight, and the ability to achieve a decisive result became increasingly illusive (Donovan et al. 25). As Walter Mills notes, war had begun to lose its one redeeming virtue, the ability to reach a rapid decision (124–125).

MANEUVER AND COMMAND AND CONTROL

Command and control in the Mexican War were based largely on line-of-sight signaling, couriers, and audible signals. Thus when George Pickett led the charge at Chapultepec carrying the unit colors, he was not just setting a brave example but facilitating command and control by giving the Eighth Infantry a rallying marker for the advance.

Indeed, under the limited means of command and control available in the era, the close physical proximity of leaders to the fighting was critical. Maurice Matloff writes that at Buena Vista,

> [p]erhaps the greatest contribution to the victory had been Zachary Taylor himself. Stationed all day conspicuously in the center of the battle hunched on his horse "Old Whitey," with one leg hooked over the pommel of his saddle, disregarding two Mexican bullets that ripped through his coat, and occasionally rising in his stirrups to shout encouragement, he was an inspiration to his men, who swore by him. Under such a leader they felt that defeat was impossible. (172–173)

But the need for the commander's physical presence also indicated the era's difficulty in controlling what was beyond one's field of view.

Offensive operations in the Civil War remained hard to coordinate and even harder to control. Civil War commanders who tried to follow the example of Scott's Mexican War turning movements and attack the enemy's flank and

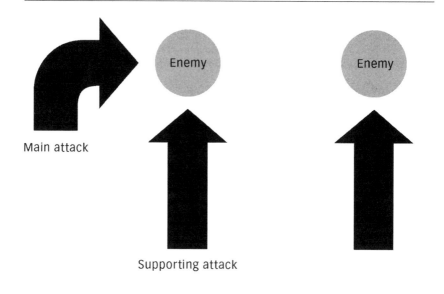

Main attack

Supporting attack

ENVELOPMENT   **FRONTAL ATTACK**

Difficulties in controlling more complicated envelopments led many Civil War commanders to continue to rely on frontal attacks.

rear often experienced frustration because of the command and control difficulties. The command and control system necessary to coordinate multiple attacks at different locations was quite beyond the ability of many Civil War commanders. Chris Gabel concludes that "most often . . . Civil War battles [involving simultaneous attacks] quickly devolved into a confusing blur of regimental attacks and withdrawals completely beyond the control of higher headquarters" (*Vicksburg* 38–39). This fact led Civil War armies to repeatedly attack each other frontally, exchanging higher casualties for easier execution.

Even simpler efforts at increased tactical sophistication, such as expanding the traditional close-order formations, were thwarted by the problems of command and control. T. Harry Williams writes, "Many officers would have been willing to experiment with a more dispersed formation if they thought they could keep command over their men, but the difficulty of maintaining communication baffled them" (T. Williams, *History* 194). In the absence of radios, Civil War commanders were forced to rely on visual signals such as unit colors and drums and bugles to conptrol their formations. This requirement would prove to be a significantly limiting factor.

MANEUVER AND TRANSPORTATION

The Mexican War would present the army with longer supply lines than it had previously ever experienced. At the beginning of the war, the principal American field force commanded by Zachary Taylor was stationed on the lower Rio Grande. Its main depot was at Point Isabel on the Gulf of Mexico, about 9 miles north of the mouth of the river and 600 miles from New Orleans, the source of its supplies. After Taylor advanced into Mexico, he established another depot 300 miles up the Rio Grande at Camargo.

These long-distance transportation problems were met in part by steamboats, and for this reason the Mexican War is known as "the first steamboat war." The Quartermaster Department used steamboats to carry troops and supplies down the Mississippi River to New Orleans. It bought light-draft Mississippi River steamboats to run up the shallow Rio Grande to Camargo. Lieutenant George Meade described these vessels as "mere shells," certainly never meant to be oceangoing. Nonetheless, most made the voyage over 600 miles of "tempestuous sea" to Port Isabel. Brigadier General Thomas Jesup, the quartermaster general of the army, proposed the construction of a military railroad to supply Taylor's army, but a lack of funds ensured the project never came to fruition (Stauffer 3). Instead, it would fall to the Civil War to become "the first great railroad war" (Weigley, *History* 222).

On the eve of the Civil War, there were generally three railroad systems in the United States. The first was an east-west system running north of the Ohio River and connecting the Old Northwest and the trans-Mississippi West with the East. The North retained control of this rail system, along with the northern rivers, canals, and Great Lakes, to form a high-capacity transportation network that allowed rapid movement of troops, supplies, and produce between the eastern and western theaters. The second system was a less efficient one along the eastern seaboard that connected Chattanooga, Atlanta, and Richmond. The prewar lines between Richmond and Washington and the east-west lines throughout Virginia were used by both sides during the war. The third system ran parallel to the Mississippi River and aided armies operating in the Mississippi Valley (Donovan et al. 5). Based on the principle of interior lines, "[a]s long as Southern railroads were available and dependable, Confederate strategists possessed the opportunity of massing and dispersing their forces much faster than the Northern invaders" (Thomas, *Confederate* 106).

In some cases, however, railroad transportation appeared to dilute some of Jomini's geometric principles, such as when the Confederate forces in the Shenandoah Valley used the Manassas Gap Railroad to unite with those around Manassas Junction in spite of having exterior lines vis-à-vis the Federals (Weigley, *American Way* 96). Railroads made geographical dispositions less relevant, and effective use of railroads by the force on exterior lines might allow it to move as fast or faster than the force on the inside. Usually this phenomenon worked against the Confederacy, where the antebellum transportation system had been designed to drain goods to such ports as New Orleans, Richmond, Norfolk, Charleston, Savannah, and Wilmington rather than to ship them across the South (Surdam 96). Few east-west lines connected the Southern system, and only one line traversed the mountain barrier connecting Richmond with Chattanooga and the Mississippi River at Memphis. Additionally, Southern railroad systems featured different gauges, which necessitated the unloading and reloading of cargo en route. Finally, of the 31,000 miles of railroad in 1860, only 9,000 were in the states of the Confederacy (Donovan et al. 5, 15).

A prime example of what the railroad could do is a case that Civil War railroad scholar Chris Gabel describes as "interior lines nullified" (*Vicksburg* 5). In September 1863, James Longstreet's 12,000-man corps traveled by rail, on interior lines, from Virginia to northern Georgia, where it reinforced Braxton Bragg's Army of Tennessee at Chickamauga. Longstreet's corps traveled some 800 miles in about twelve days. Two weeks after the Confederate victory there, in what has been called "the accomplishment par excellence of Civil War logistics," the Federal XI and XII Corps, totaling 25,000 men, traveled 1,200 miles from Virginia to the Chattanooga front, where they reinforced the defeated Army of the Cumberland (Weigley, *History* 222). This movement on exterior lines also took about twelve days, even though the distance was greater and the number of troops larger. In this case, the more efficient Union railroads demonstrated the potential to nullify Confederate interior lines (Gabel, *Railroad* 5–6).

FIREPOWER

Firepower complements maneuver by providing the destructive force essential to overcome the enemy's ability and will to fight (FM 3-0, 4-6). Scott's limited approach to war, Hunt's organization of artillery, Jackson's tactical use of artillery, and Longstreet's preference for the defense all address firepower considerations.

FIREPOWER AND RIFLES

The most common shoulder arm in the Mexican War was the flintlock musket, in spite of the fact that technical developments had made it possible to replace the flintlock with the percussion cap and therefore make muskets more reliable and serviceable in rain and snow. Indeed, in 1842 the army ceased producing flintlocks, and the Model 1841 Springfield caplock actually became the standard shoulder arm. The way the system worked was that when the weapon's hammer fell, it would strike a small brass cap that fit snugly over a nipple at the breach of the weapon. The inside of the cap was painted with a small daub of mercury fulminate, which would ignite when struck by the hammer. This sent a spark to the chamber and ignited the powder charge. The used cap could then be discarded and a new one put in place for the next firing. The percussion cap system eliminated the need to prime the weapon and achieved a much lower rate of misfires than the flintlock. However, Winfield Scott distrusted the percussion cap as being too complicated, and, because of his influence, the flintlock remained the predominant firearm when the Mexican War began. Volunteer units, however, were less traditional in embracing the new technology, and many, such as Jefferson Davis's Mississippi Rifles, were outfitted with rifles (Doughty 95; Weigley, *History* 172).

When Davis became secretary of war in 1853, he spurred the army to adopt the rifled infantry musket. By this time, a French army captain named Claude E. Minié had developed a way to load a rifled musket as easily as a smoothbore. The minié ball was a cylindro-conoidal bullet that was slightly smaller in diameter than the barrel and thus could be easily dropped down the barrel. One end, however, was hollow, and when the rifle was fired, expanding gas widened the sides of this hollow end so that the bullet would grip the rifling and create the spinning effect needed for accuracy. The United States adapted the

Model 1855 Springfield rifle to take .58-caliber minié ammunition. The difference was significant. The smoothbore musket had a range of 100 to 200 yards. The new rifle was effective from 400 to 600 yards (Weigley, *History* 190; Matloff 181; Doughty 96).

There was still one problem, and that was the loading procedures. Each soldier carried paper cartridges containing sealed powder and a minié ball. To load, the soldier would bite through the paper, pour the powder and ball down the barrel, wad the paper and drop it down the barrel, and then use his ramrod to compact the contents several times. Then he would fit the percussion cap over the small nipple at the base of the hammer, cock the hammer, take aim, and fire. A well-drilled soldier could fire two or three rounds a minute from the standing position using this procedure. Loading from the prone, however, was much slower and more difficult (Donovan et al. 25).

Breechloading rifles would solve this problem, but early models were technically unsatisfactory because gas and flame escaped from the breech. Eventually, however, a good breechloader, the Sharps, was developed at Harpers Ferry, Virginia. It was a single-shot rifle, with a carbine version being perfected in 1859 and used extensively by the cavalry. Soon the problem of sealing the gas was solved, and repeating rifles were manufactured. Eventually, a sixteen-shot Henry and a seven-shot Spencer would be used in the Civil War, but such breechloaders never represented more than a small percentage of the total individual weapons produced (Donovan et al. 25).

FIREPOWER AND ARTILLERY

Thanks to inspired secretaries of war such as John Calhoun, Lewis Cass, and Joel Poinsett, American artillery at the time of the Mexican War was outstanding. Poinsett in particular had advanced this development by sending a board of officers to Europe in 1840 to study artillery and bring back cannons from various countries for the Ordnance Department to study. As a result, in 1841, just in time for the Mexican War, a full system of American artillery was fielded (J. Eisenhower, *So Far* 379).

The 1841 system consisted entirely of smoothbore muzzleloaders: six- and twelve-pounder guns; twelve-, twenty-four-, and thirty-two-pounder howitzers; and twelve-pounder mountain howitzers. Bronze was the standard construction material for all field pieces. A battery usually consisted of six pieces—

four guns and two howitzers. The guns fired solid shot, shell, spherical case, grapeshot, and canister. The six-pounder gun was the primary field piece in the Mexican War and had an effective range of 1,523 yards (Gabel, *Vicksburg* 25).

The role of the artillery in Mexico was absolutely pivotal. On the eve of the war in 1845, Scott wrote a tactical manual extolling the virtues of the new mobile artillery batteries being employed in France and Great Britain. Pursuant to this model, the United States had organized one company in each artillery regiment as light, or "flying," artillery, designed for use with infantry. Indeed, at Palo Alto, Weigley describes the artillery as "maneuvering with almost the flexibility of cavalry, standing beside or sometimes in front of the infantry" (*History* 184).

Palo Alto is an example of artillery in the defense, and Mexican War artillery was frequently used defensively to blast advancing enemy lines with canister and then withdraw when the enemy got within musket range. But the Mexican War is also replete with examples of the use of artillery in an offensive role. Napoleonic tactics required the artillery to pound the enemy's guns and infantry at relatively short range. In this manner, the artillery would create a breach in the enemy's defenses through which the friendly infantry could pass (Weigley, *History* 184). This was possible because of artillery's advantage in "stand-off." The infantry musket of the Mexican War was inaccurate, even against massed targets, beyond 100 yards, while artillery was extremely deadly firing canister at about 400 yards. With such a differential in their favor, Mexican War artillerists were able to leisurely work their guns without much fear of infantry muskets endangering them (Gabel, *Vicksburg* 35).

This would all change with the Civil War, however. The 1841 system based on the six-pounder had become obsolete, and in 1857 a new, more versatile twelve-pounder gun-howitzer appeared on the scene. This Model 1857 was a multipurpose piece designed to replace existing guns and howitzers. It could fire canister and shell like the twelve-pounder howitzer and solid shot at an effective range of 1,680 yards like the twelve-pounder gun (Gabel, *Vicksburg* 25).

Like its Mexican War predecessors, the Model 1857 was a smoothbore. Although rifled artillery pieces had been developed, they did not have the dramatic impact that rifled muskets did. Although rifled artillery provided greater range and accuracy, such guns proved somewhat less reliable and slower to load than smoothbores. More important, the canister load of the rifle under-performed that of the smoothbore. The most common rifled guns were the ten-pounder Parrott and the Rodman, or three-inch, ordnance rifle (Gabel, *Vicksburg* 26).

But even rifled artillery pieces were unable to restore artillery to its Napoleonic prominence in the attack. Against protected defenders, the artillery could not get close enough to have the desired effect with canister without exposing the gunners to the long-range fire of the defenders' rifles. Furthermore, the increased range of cannons provided no real advantage in the broken and wooded terrain common on so many Civil War battlefields. Indeed, in places like the Wilderness, Lee consciously chose to give battle in restricted terrain that would negate Grant's artillery advantage (Catton, *Glory Road* 285–289). In the Civil War, both technology and terrain cost artillery the assumed stand-off advantage over the infantry it enjoyed in Mexico. Consequently, most successful Civil War artillery actions would be defensive rather than offensive (Gabel, *Vicksburg* 37; Weigley, *History* 236).

LEADERSHIP

Leadership provides purpose, direction, and motivation. It is the most dynamic element of combat power (FM 3-0, 4-7). Perhaps for this reason, its representation is the broadest in this study. Kearney's reckless courage, Pope's attitude toward civilians, Meade's caution, the Federal Jefferson Davis's temper, the Confederate Jefferson Davis's self-reliance, Hooker's administrative skill, Sherman's personal growth, Halleck's calling as an executive manager rather than a field commander, Thomas's unflappable perseverance, Bragg's martinet style, Winder's wartime governance, Pillow's cowardice, Pemberton's inflexibility, Hill's criticism, and Armistead's compassion are all related to leadership.

LEADERSHIP AND SPAN OF CONTROL

The Mexican War represented the first time American soldiers were organized into divisions. Russell Weigley describes divisions as "the somewhat autonomous armies that had appeared with the growth of armies during the French Revolution" (*History* 182). Napoleon had created these organizations to facilitate his flanking maneuvers (Weigley, *American Way* 75). Indeed, the turning movement would be extremely prevalent in the Mexican War. However, finding suitable generals to lead these new divisions would be difficult. William Worth would show some qualities of brilliance, but his quarrelsome, erratic, and self-centered personality would limit his usefulness. David Twigg's lack of sophistication prevented him from advancing beyond the blunt and costly frontal assault. John Wool was perhaps the steadiest of the division commanders, but even he "demonstrated no capacities that were strikingly large" (Weigley, *History* 182).

The difficulty in finding capable senior commanders was partially offset by the fact that the numbers involved in any one battle in Mexico were always relatively small. Taylor commanded about 6,000 men at Monterrey and less than 5,000 at Buena Vista. Scott landed with about 10,000 men at Vera Cruz and led less than 700 more out of Puebla on the march to Mexico City. The terrain in Mexico further helped to keep the scope of combat small. Factors such as heavy chaparral growth at Resaca de la Palma and street fighting at Monterey served to break larger battles up into multiple fragmentary actions (Weigley, *History* 183–184). The result of these factors in Mexico would be an increased importance of the junior officer corps, and this cohort of junior officers in Mexico would grow into the senior commanders of the Civil War.

But issues with span of control nonetheless plagued the Civil War generals. Mexico had simply not prepared the developing military commander for anything comparable to the size of the armies that would require leadership in the Civil War. At First Manassas, Irvin McDowell commanded 35,000 men. In the two days of fighting at Shiloh, the Confederates suffered 10,699 casualties and the Federals 13,047, numbers that both rivaled or exceeded the size of Scott's entire army. McClellan moved 121,500 men to Fort Monroe, Virginia, for his Peninsula Campaign. Lee led some 70,000 men into Pennsylvania for his Gettysburg Campaign. Grant attacked Lee with 119,000 men at the Wilderness. These were numbers unimaginable in the Mexican War, where Scott led less than 13,000 men. By Civil War standards, Scott's entire army "would scarcely have made a respectable army corps" (Doughty 92). As important a role as West Pointers would play in the Civil War, not a single one had previously controlled as large a unit as a brigade, and only a few had handled a regiment (Donald 37).

Providing senior leadership for such large numbers of men would stress both the Confederate and Federal armies. Lincoln would cycle through the likes of McDowell, McClellan, Pope, McClellan again, Burnside, Hooker, and Meade before settling on Grant. Lee would be forced to reorganize his army from two to three corps after the death of Stonewall Jackson left him with a leadership shortage. Many generals on both sides would be forced to assume responsibilities that far exceeded their talents.

Nonetheless, the generals' lack of familiarity with handling large troop formations did little to dampen their desire for greater numbers. The strong influence of the Jominian doctrine of concentration led many generals to believe winning the war called for one big effort at one time in one theater. Much of the apparent caution of every Federal general in the first years of the war can be attributed to his belief that he needed more troops. McClellan on the Peninsula is a classic example. But this attitude was in conflict with Lincoln's non-Jominian approach, and it was not until the arrival of Grant that Lincoln would find a soul mate in developing a comprehensive, coordinated strategy (Donald 45–46).

LEADERSHIP AND WEST POINT

If Jomini was the principal influence on American strategic thought, the man who gave Jomini his most important American audience was Sylvanus Thayer. In 1817, Thayer replaced Captain Alden Partridge as superintendent of West Point and began reversing the damage Partridge had done. Thayer broadened and standardized the curriculum, established a system to measure class standing, organized classes around small sections, tightened cadet discipline, created the office of commandant of cadets, and improved military training.

By the time of the Mexican War, Thayer's reforms had produced a generation of men who would fill the junior officers' ranks in Mexico. These lieutenants and captains stood in sharp contrast to the older officers, who had not benefited from a systematic military education and training. The influence of Thayer and West Point was readily apparent. Mexican War historian John Eisenhower assesses that "Taylor had inherited an excellent set of junior officers, largely products of Sylvanus Thayer's teaching methods at West Point" (*So Far* 35). Winfield Scott called his West Pointers his "little cabinet," and this fine collection of officers allowed Scott to assemble what Weigley terms "the first American field staff to approach adequacy" (*History* 185). Scott was unwavering in his acknowledgment of West Pointers, declaring, "I give it as my fixed opinion that but for our graduated cadets the war between the United States and Mexico might, and probably would, have lasted some four or five years, with, in its first half, more defeats than victories falling to our share, whereas in two campaigns we conquered a great country and a peace without the loss of a single battle or skirmish" (Cullum 11).

Thayer also used West Point to stimulate a systematic American study of war, which sought to synchronize the diverse components of maritime and land-based activity into a coherent American strategy. To do so, Thayer borrowed heavily from Europe, especially France. Key among these European theorists was Jomini.

Jomini's ideas were present in a summary contained in Captain J. M. O'Connor's translation of S. F. Gay de Vernon's *Treatise on the Science of War and Fortifications*, as well as in the teachings of Dennis Hart Mahan, a protégé of Thayer's who joined the West Point faculty in 1832 and became the academy's principal instructor of warfare. For Mahan, nothing remained to be learned about the art of war that had not been discovered by Napoleon, and his students such as Henry Halleck were profoundly influenced by Jomini. Halleck published *Elements of Military Art and Science* in 1846, a treatise that would have a significant impact on the Civil War. In fact, Halleck would use his time aboard ship en route to Mexican War service in California to translate Jomini's *Life of Napoleon* (Weigley, *American Way* 81–87). Halleck's *Elements* was never adopted as a West Point text, but it was probably the most widely read strategic treatise among American military officers (Doughty 97). The end result was that "every West Point general in the [Civil War] had been exposed to Jomini's ideas, either directly, by reading Jomini's writings or abridgments or expositions of them; or indirectly, by hearing them in the classroom or perusing the works of Jomini's American disciples" (Donald 37–38).

LEADERSHIP AND VOLUNTEERS

The Mexican War manpower policy was largely based on political considerations. Geographic enthusiasm for the war was generally confined to the South, because many Northerners saw the war as veiled attempt to expand slavery. Given the soft support for the war, especially in the northeastern states,

President Polk decided to avoid any heavy reliance on the militia. Instead, he opted to double the size of the Regular Army and raise 50,000 volunteers, most of whom would be drawn from Southern states (Doughty 84).

There were numerous discipline problems among the volunteers, involving both individuals and entire units. Much of the misbehavior was directed at Mexican civilians (Bauer 83). Weigley attempts to provide a balanced assessment of the volunteers' performance, noting that "some volunteer regiments occasionally fought less than well in Mexico, such as the unhappy 2nd Indiana at Buena Vista, to provide grist for the mills of the Uptonian historians who were determined to find little that was good to say about them. But in this war another kind of example was easier to find. If Taylor could not have won Buena Vista without his Regular artillery, neither could he have won it without his volunteers" (*History* 187). Nonetheless, many contemporary professional soldiers were scathing in their criticism of volunteers. George McClellan wrote his sister that "the government has placed Genl Taylor in a very dangerous situation. . . . [M]ay the Lord deliver him, for it is pretty certain that the volunteers won't. . . . [I]f 7000 regulars had been at Genl Taylor's disposal on the Rio Grande, the war would in all probability have been finished at one blow" (Rafuse 42).

Volunteers would also form a critical part of the Civil War armies. Service in Mexico would be formative for leaders because, as Alfred Bill observes, it was there that so many Federal and Confederate commanders would gain "some knowledge of the virtues and shortcomings of the American volunteer soldier, who was to make up the bulk of the armies they were to lead against each other" (ix–x). Indeed, George Meade and John Reynolds exemplify those who would carry their negative perception of the volunteer soldier in Mexico into their Civil War service.

Two days after the inauguration of President Lincoln, the Congress of the Confederate States of America, faced with the problem of building an army from scratch, voted that 100,000 volunteers be enlisted for one year. Soon the Confederates began enlisting soldiers for the duration of the war as well as offering the one-year enlistees various inducements to reenlist for two additional years. Nonetheless, in early 1862 it became apparent that such measures would not meet the Confederacy's manpower needs, and the South turned to the drastic measure of conscription (Weigley, *History* 198).

The Union faced less drastic circumstances, most notably because it retained the prewar enlisted strength of the Regular Army virtually intact, and therefore was able to proceed more slowly. On the day after the evacuation of Fort Sumter, Lincoln used the Militia Act of 1792 to call upon the states to provide 75,000 militia for three months of federal service. The country's militia institutions provided a valuable stopgap measure in the Union's time of crisis (Weigley, *History* 199).

The Federal defeat at First Manassas dispelled most hopes of a short war, and the Union, like the Confederacy, turned to more long-term manpower solutions. On May 3, Lincoln called for 42,034 volunteers to serve for three years unless sooner discharged and increased the Regular Army's strength by 22,714. The Union response exceeded Lincoln's request astronomically. By July 1, Secretary of War Simon Cameron reported 310,000 men under arms. On July 4, Lincoln requested 400,000 three-year volunteers. Congress responded by authorizing 400,000. One day after First Manassas, Congress authorized another 500,000 volunteers, thus bringing the total authorization to a volunteer army of 1,000,000 men. Eventually, some 700,000 men enlisted under the two acts (Weigley, *History* 200).

Still, there were manpower needs, and in 1862 the Union, like the Confederacy, resorted to conscription. At first conscription was managed at the state level, but in 1863 the Enrollment Act established federal conscription. The draft proved to be an inefficient system for raising troops because of exemptions, substitutions, commutations, and expenses. In the end, only 6 percent of the total Union manpower was raised by conscription. Its greatest contribution seems to have been to encourage voluntary enlistments (Donovan et al. 23).

LEADERSHIP AND POLITICAL CONSIDERATIONS

Historical analysis has been unkind to Polk as a wartime president, but to be fair, Polk had to contend with a complicated situation. To be sure, he was plagued by his own unabashed partisanship, but beyond his control Polk also was faced with the problem of active presidential aspirations of his generals. Both Taylor and Scott freely intermingled military and political campaigning. To make matters worse, both were Whigs, so their ambitions stimulated the Democrat Polk's natural tendency to allow politics to influence war making (Weigley, *History* 177).

Taylor quickly emerged as a Whig favorite and personally became enchanted by the prospects of becoming president. Caught up in this ambition, Taylor began to see every disagreement with the War Department as evidence of a Democratic plot to keep him from the White House. Taylor's sensitivity served as a catalyst for administration distrust, and soon Polk and his cabinet did begin to actively work to squash Taylor's political prospects. As Taylor continued to enjoy one battlefield victory after another, Polk decided that political expediency necessitated that someone else would have to lead the final drive to Mexico City (Weigley, *History* 177). Ulysses Grant sums up the situation in his *Memoirs*:

> The administration had indeed a most embarrassing problem to solve. It was engaged in a war of conquest which must be carried to a successful issue, or the political object would be unattained. Yet all the capable officers of the requisite rank belonged to the opposition, and the man selected for his lack of political ambition had himself become a prominent candidate for the Presidency. It was necessary to destroy his chances promptly. The problem was to do this without the loss of conquest and without permitting another general of the same political party to acquire like popularity. (57)

Scott was the obvious alternative to Taylor, but Scott presented just as much a political problem for Polk as Taylor did. Thus Polk tried to delay the inevitable as long as possible while exploring every option available. Whomever was selected would likely emerge a war hero and presidential candidate, because, as Grant wrote, "nothing so popularizes a candidate for high civil positions as military victories" (56). Polk obviously favored a Democratic choice, but his options were limited.

Among the Democratic major generals, Robert Patterson was unsuitable because of his foreign birth, and William Butler was an unknown quantity as an army commander. John Wool had been the third-ranking officer in the prewar army and was a Democrat, but for some reason appears to have escaped consideration. Polk went so far in his effort to avoid Scott as to consider the rather imaginative option of Thomas Hart Benton, a senator and a proponent of the Vera Cruz landing. On November 10, Benton approached Polk with the innovative solution that he be appointed lieutenant general and given command of the landing. While such a move may have been politically appealing to Polk, appointing Benton to the post would require congressional approval, and, as Congress was not in session, this would have taken too long. Having explored all other options, Polk reluctantly was forced to give the command to Scott (Bauer 235).

Scott and Polk had already had a tense relationship. Grant records, "The fact is, the administration of Mr. Polk made every preparation to disgrace Scott, or, to speak more correctly, to drive him to such desperation that he would disgrace himself" (57). It appears Scott soon came to agree with this assessment, and he joined Taylor in believing himself to be the target of an administration conspiracy. Scott expressed this sentiment as he departed for Mexico, stating he was threatened by "a fire upon my rear, from Washington, and the fire, in front, from the Mexicans" (Weigley, *History* 178).

The situation inevitably degenerated, and neither Polk, Scott, nor Taylor acquitted himself particularly nobly. To exacerbate the situation, Scott had to contend with the likes of Gideon Pillow, who had risen to the post of division commander almost exclusively based on his political connections to Polk and who now viewed himself as his former law partner's "representative" in the army (J. Eisenhower, *Agent* 254).

The problems Scott experienced with Pillow exemplify the political machinations of the Mexican War command climate. On two occasions Scott would try to discipline Pillow, only to have Polk directly or indirectly intervene. Such a spectacle would have a profound effect on the junior officers who witnessed it. Professional officers generally strived to maintain political neutrality. Taylor and Scott went so far as to never vote while they were in active service (Weigley, *History* 189). Nonetheless, the imposition of political intrigue in military matters undoubtedly affected those who observed it. Of particular note, George McClellan would gain a contempt for politicians that would negatively impact his relations with President Lincoln during the Civil War.

Political considerations would also affect military decisions in the Civil War. The shortage of suitable professional senior officers, the need to placate valuable constituencies, and the need to build national cohesion led both Lincoln and Davis to appoint many political generals. Pillow, for example, would resurface as a Confederate general. The political gains of such tactics notwithstanding, many of these appointees, including Pillow, proved disappointing on the Civil War battlefield.

Lincoln and Davis also had to make political decisions regarding their nations at war. Lincoln was much more willing to take an authoritative approach in this area. His administration suspended the writ of habeas corpus where necessary and held, at one time or another, an estimated 13,000 political prisoners. Censorship was also much more common in the North than in the South (Donald 87; Doughty 173).

In contrast, David Donald assesses that the Confederacy "Died of Democracy" because of the Southern people's steadfast insistence to retain their democratic liberties in wartime (90). The Confederacy owed its very existence to the notion of states' rights, and President Davis would meet strong opposition to any efforts at nationalization. He was continually challenged by locally minded governors such as Joseph Brown of Georgia, who condemned Davis as attempting "fearful strides towards a centralized government with unlimited powers" (Donald 88). Even Davis's vice president, Alexander Stephens, undercut Davis's authority. It was Davis's dilemma that seemingly rational responses to the emergencies of war would destroy the political philosophy upon which his nation existed (Thomas, *Confederate* 196).

But Davis was not alone in having to fend off political challenges. Lincoln had to deal with antiwar Copperheads, draft riots, emancipation, rabid Republicans, and the Joint Committee on the Conduct of the War. Ironically, just as Polk had to worry about the political aspirations of his generals in Mexico, Lincoln would be challenged in the 1864 presidential election by his former general George McClellan.

LEADERSHIP AND OBJECTIVE

Carl von Clausewitz is often quoted as explaining that "war is merely the continuation of politics by other means" (Clausewitz 87), and this assessment does much to explain the objectives of the United States in Mexico. Expansion, as defined by the fulfillment of Manifest Destiny, was the linchpin of American foreign policy at the time, and the United States had specific designs on Texas, California, and New Mexico. The United States also had forces in place to effect these plans, including Taylor's army along the Texas border, John C. Frémont's "exploring party" in California, Stephen Kearney just a short march from New Mexico, and navy units off of California. When war was declared, it did not take the United States long to gain firm control of much of northern Mexico as well as California and New Mexico. At this point, Polk had figured that the Mexican government would sue for peace. When this calculation proved inaccurate, a new campaign, Scott's drive to the capital, would be required to compel surrender (Doughty 84–86).

Scott's objective was very defined. The territorial gains the United States had sought at the beginning of the war were already in or imminently in American hands by the time Scott's campaign began. Thus Scott's objective was to be a limited one: to convince the Mexican government of the futility of continuing the war. Accordingly, Scott did not ever consider it part of his purpose to destroy the Mexican army. Instead, he settled on a completely political strategy. By capturing the capital of Mexico City, Scott calculated that he could so disrupt Mexican political life as to paralyze the country and compel a surrender. His objective then became to capture Mexico City as quickly as possible with the lowest number of casualties (Weigley, *American Way* 73–74).

Scott would carry this same philosophy of limited war into the Civil War by proposing the time-consuming but low-casualty-producing Anaconda Plan. Many of Scott's junior officers such as McClellan would also bring a very limited objective approach to the Civil War, and the strategy of conciliation to the Confederacy was especially common at the beginning of the war (Rafuse 186). Times, however, had changed, and such a patient and deliberate strategy became unpopular because it appeared to play into the Confederacy's hands. For its part, the Confederacy was in no hurry. Its objective was merely to maintain the status quo, to convince the North that it was not worth its while to continue fighting and to accept Confederate independence. The Federal objective to restore the Union was much more complicated. It would lead the North to approach the Civil War as a total war in order to gain victory, yet at the same time Lincoln would always have to bear in mind that too much damage inflicted on the South and its people would imperil the reunification that was his objective.

In many ways Lincoln, the military novice, was far ahead of his generals in coming to grips with his strategic problem. In spite of strong objections by the likes of McClellan, Lincoln realized that the Emancipation Proclamation, aside from its moral imperative, would take the war to a new level in terms of objective. Now the North was not just fighting to restore what Northerners be-lieved had never legitimately been separated, but instead fighting an enlight-ened crusade to end slavery. The total nature of the war was further elevated with the ascendancy of Ulysses Grant, who, in sharp contrast to Scott, believed the war could not be won without heavy loss of life. Through a strategy of an-nihilation, Grant made both the Confederate army and its resources his ob-jective. Grant's lieutenant William Sherman fully understand the new totality, declaring, "[W]e are not only fighting hostile armies, but a hostile people, and must make old and young, rich and poor, feel the hard hand of war, as well as organized armies." In terms of objective, the Civil War would far outstrip the Mexican War and take the American way of war to an entirely new level (Weigley, *American Way* 128–152).

PROTECTION

Protection is "the preservation of the fighting potential of a force so the com-mander can apply maximum force at the decisive time and place" (FM 3-0, 4-8). Grant's "cutting loose" from his base, Thomas's logistical caution, Long-street's use of defensive fieldworks, and Pemberton's defense of Vicksburg all address protection.

PROTECTION AND STRENGTH OF DEFENSE

Most Civil War commanders entered the Civil War well versed in the Mexican War view that the offensive was the decisive form of battle. Indeed, in Mexico even frontal assaults against smoothbore muskets were successful and had left many commanders with an exaggerated view of their potential (Doughty 91). However, technological advances in terms of the improved range and accuracy of the rifle had in fact changed this assumption. Nonetheless, many command-ers continued to employ the tactical offensive long after it was clear that the defensive was superior. Part of this may have been slow learning, but the of-fense did continue to have its advantages. It allowed the attacker to maintain the initiative and removed the uncontrollable requirement levied by the defen-sive of being dependent on the attacker's attacking at a point of the defender's choosing and continuing to attack until badly defeated. Although this situation did occur often in the Civil War, it was not something defending commanders could count on. Consequently, few commanders chose to rely on the protective strength of the defensive so long as they had the option to attack (Gabel, *Vicksburg* 37).

PROTECTION AND ENGINEERING

Sylvanus Thayer to a significant degree had modeled West Point after the French military schools, which greatly stressed engineering. Thus, at the time of the Mexican War, many officers were well versed in military engineering and proved very adept in selecting and fortifying field positions, so much so that Weigley asserts, "It was in the Mexican War that American . . . engineering, hitherto entrusted so often to foreign officers, at last came of age" (*History* 185).

Buena Vista would exemplify the protective value of terrain. Rather than engage the Mexicans in the open, Taylor withdrew to a naturally strong position near the Buena Vista hacienda, where a latticework of hills, precipitous slopes, tangled arroyos, and deep ravines partially outnumbered the Mexicans' numerical advantage (Bauer 209–210; Doughty 86). In addition to these natural benefits, the thick walls of the hacienda provided solid protection and were useful in repulsing repeated Mexican attacks (Bauer 215).

Buena Vista represented Santa Anna's sole offensive campaign of the war, but the Mexican general had little success in using the strength of the defense to his advantage. His attempt to defend from the castle and other buildings at Chapultepec is a good example. Santa Anna's efforts to improve the positions suffered from manpower shortages, and he never completed his preparations. Nonetheless, the complex presented obstacles to the Americans in the form of a high stone wall, an aqueduct whose arches had been filled in with masonry, a fosse, a minefield, and various breastworks and redans. Such a seemingly complex system, however, was successfully breached by Voltigeur companies led by future Confederate general Joe Johnston and artillery led by future Confederate general Thomas Jackson. Santa Anna voiced his frustration with the repeated inability of defenses to provide protection against such offensive breaching by exclaiming, "I believe if we were to plant our batteries in Hell the damned Yankees would take them from us" (Bauer 313–318). Santa Anna's lament reflected the reality that at this point in the evolution of warfare technology, the limited ranges of weapons allowed attackers to close with defenders and blast holes in their fortifications with relative impunity. Such would not be the case in the Civil War.

As previously noted, the development of the rifle altered the relationship between the offense and the defense. Now the defender, especially when protected by breastworks, could destroy the attackers as they advanced across open terrain. Consequently, protected defensive positions would become critical in the Civil War.

For example, at Fredericksburg, Confederates took positions on a sunken road behind a four-foot-high stone wall. The Federals made six major assaults, fourteen in total, against the nearly impregnable position. All failed, resulting in 12,500 casualties compared to only 5,500 for the Confederates (Doughty 153–154; Donovan et al. 200–201).

At Fredericksburg, the protection took the form of an existing wall, but elsewhere engineers would lay out and infantry would prepare similarly strong defenses. Companies prepared breastworks of earth and logs to cover their fronts. The procedure was to fell and trim trees and then roll the logs into a line to form a timber revetment usually four feet high. This structure was then banked with earth from a ditch dug to its front. The result was a sloping parapet about seven to ten feet thick at the top and an additional three feet thick at the bottom. On top of the revetment was a line of head logs positioned to leave a horizontal loophole about three inches wide through which to fire. The trees and bushes in front of the breastwork were then felled outward to create an obstacle that sometimes was augmented by a cheval-de-frise, or a sharpened palisade. The drill became such a matter of routine that a company could cover itself within an hour of halting, even without engineer support (Hart 262–263).

As William Sherman pressed Joe Johnston from Dalton to Atlanta, Georgia, Johnston would repeatedly withdraw to such prepared positions to block Sherman's path (Grant 381). Johnston would dispatch his engineers ahead of his infantry to locate and lay out his next defensive position. Sherman's usual policy was to try to outmaneuver these positions and envelop Johnston, but at Kennesaw Mountain Sherman tried a frontal attack. The results were predictable. Sherman lost about 3,000 casualties. The Confederates lost at most a third of that number. Johnston explains his success by writing, "More of their [the

Federals'] best soldiers lay dead and wounded than the number of British veterans that fell in General [Andrew] Jackson's celebrated battle of New Orleans, the foremost dead lying against our breastworks, they retired—unsuccessful—because they had encountered *intrenched* infantry unsurpassed by that of Napoleon's Old Guard, or that which followed Wellington into France, out of Spain" (343).

Johnston's respect for the strength of the entrenched defense is unmistakable, and the results of Kennesaw speak for themselves. However, Sherman was able ultimately to reach Atlanta. One observer concludes, "At Kennesaw Sherman learned again the cost of assaulting an enemy behind earthworks. For Johnston the lesson learned had been evident since the beginning of the campaign: earthworks can delay but not defeat a determined enemy who can maneuver" (Luvaas 191).

PROTECTION AND LOGISTICS

In Mexico, by and large, the armies had to provide their own subsistence because of the great distances involved. Provisions were either purchased or requisitioned by commissary officers accompanying the army or more informally gathered by the troops. Civilian sutlers had accompanied American armies since the Revolutionary War, and this practice continued in Mexico (Weigley, *History* 180).

Securing lengthy logistical lines of communication against guerrilla attack was a resource-intensive undertaking for Scott as he marched to Mexico City. To counter this problem, Scott boldly decided to reduce his fixed line of supply and live off the land. Ulysses Grant would employ a similar tactic in the Vicksburg Campaign.

More typically, and even to a large extent in the Vicksburg Campaign, the Civil War logistical system relied on the depot and the wagon. Matériel would flow from the factory to base depots as directed by bureau chiefs. From there, supplies were shipped to advanced depots, usually in a city on a major transportation artery within the rear of the department. While campaigning, armies would establish temporary advanced depots that could be serviced by river or rail. From these locations, wagons carried supplies forward to the field units.

Civil War logistical trains were just as vulnerable as Scott's were in Mexico. The standard was for wagons to be drawn by a six-mule team. If a corps wagon train was using the six-mule teams, it would be spread out from five to eight miles, depending on road conditions, weather, and terrain. Under optimal conditions, a wagon could haul 4,000 pounds, but only half that over difficult terrain. Oftentimes herds of beef accompanied the wagon trains to provide fresh, but tough, meat for the troops. While the meat was a welcome part of the diet, the herds slowed and complicated movement.

Sustenance for the animals was a critical concern. Each animal required up to twenty pounds of hay and grain a day to stay healthy and productive. Wagons traveling more than a day's journey from the depot had to carry excessive amounts of animal forage. If full forage was to be carried, the required number of wagons rose dramatically. This problem was partially alleviated by the practice of foraging—collecting provisions from the countryside, sometimes with, and sometimes without, command authorization (Gabel, *Vicksburg* 47–48).

PROTECTION AND MEDICAL SERVICES

Disease has always been a major killer in wartime, and much of the medical effort in the modern army is aimed at prevention through proper field sanitation. Such practices were far from the norm in Mexico, especially in Taylor's army. Taylor had slack sanitation discipline and took few medical precautions. Consequently, 1,500 of his men died in the camp at Camargo in August 1846 as Taylor made preparations for his invasion. By the time Taylor was ready to march, almost every volunteer regiment had a third to half of its men on the sick list (Weigley, *History* 181). Nonbattlefield fatalities were by far the biggest cause of death in Mexico, where 1,192 men were killed in action and another 529 died of wounds, compared to 11,155 who died from disease, accidents, executions, and other miscellaneous causes (Bauer 397).

Such medical inattention was common in most national armies at the time of the Mexican War, but the medical service in the Crimean War was so atrocious that reforms were initiated. Inspired in part by the work of Florence Nightingale in the Crimea, the U.S. Sanitary Commission, a civilian organization dedicated to improving medical care in the army, sprang up almost as soon as the Civil War began. The Sanitary Commission's members were largely middle-class humanitarian women backed by wealthy and influential philanthropists. Its work included raising money for medical supplies, pressing for bureaucratic reforms, and circulating an unprecedented guidebook titled *Rules for Preserving the Health of the Soldier*. The Sanitary Commission was able to influence the War Department to issue a general order providing for women nurses in military hospitals, though not in camps or on the march. These nurses served under the formidable Dorothea Dix. Later, Clara Barton developed an ambulance service independent of Dix's organization and was given special permission to travel with the Army of the Potomac (Weigley, *History* 225).

The disastrous experience at First Manassas led Surgeon Jonathan Letterman to establish a system for medical evacuation and treatment. The system called for the consolidation of field hospitals at the division level, decentralization of medical control of ambulances to the regimental level, and centralization of medical control of ambulances at all levels. Under this structure, a battlefield casualty was usually evacuated from the front line to a regimental holding area immediately to the rear, where he would receive treatment. From there, wagons and ambulances carried the wounded to a division field hospital, normally within a mile from the battle lines. The more seriously wounded were evacuated further by wagon, rail, or water to general hospitals located in towns along lines of communication in the rear areas.

The Confederate system was similar, but Confederate hospitals were often consolidated at the brigade rather than the division level. The Confederate system also had a different control structure. Unlike their Federal counterparts, who had control over all medical activities within an army area, Confederate army medical directors had no authority beyond their own brigade or division hospitals. Instead, a separate medical director for large hospitals was responsible for evacuation and control. The two directors relied on close cooperation to resolve any issues.

In both the Federal and Confederate systems, commanders tried to discourage soldiers from leaving the battle line to escort wounded soldiers to the rear. Instead, a dedicated detail, often comprised of bandsmen, was supposed to perform litter and ambulance duty. Nonetheless, especially in ill-disciplined units, it was common practice for soldiers to leave their positions to evacuate comrades.

Ambulances were specially designed two- or four-wheel carts with springs to limit jolts, but rough roads could still make even short trips agonizing. Field hospitals were located near a water source, in proximity to buildings that could supplement tents, and out of range of enemy fire. The most common surgical procedure at the field hospitals was amputations. Approximately 70 percent of Civil War wounds occurred in the extremities, where the soft minié ball would shatter any bone it hit. Amputation was the best technique then available to limit the chance of serious infection. Federal doctors generally had sufficient chloroform, morphine, and other drugs to provide some relief, but Confederate surgeons often experienced critical shortages. Throughout the war, the simple lack of knowledge about the true causes of disease and infection led to many more deaths than direct battlefield action (Gabel, *Vicksburg* 63–64).

INFORMATION

Information allows the commander to understand the situation and make decisions. It "enhances leadership and magnifies the effects of maneuver, firepower, and protection" (FM 3-0, 4-10). McClellan's insatiable desire for intelligence, Lee's use of reconnaissance, Slidell's efforts at diplomatic persuasion, Pemberton's paralyzing confusion, and the general knowledge nearly all the Civil War generals had of each other from their previous experiences in Mexico and elsewhere are examples of information.

INFORMATION AND INTELLIGENCE

In Mexico, the army was understandably unprepared to fight on foreign soil. Little was known about Mexican capabilities or even the geography and climate. Maps were so scarce that Scott had to plan the Vera Cruz campaign based on sketches made by a former United States consul at the city. To find out geographic and climatic information, Scott consulted two men he knew to have traveled in Mexico. Once in Mexico, Scott did benefit from a company of spies organized by Ethan Allen Hitchcock. These members of the Mexican civilian population and deserters worked together with a network of agents in Mexico City to provide much useful information (Weigley, *History* 179, 185–186).

But Scott's greatest intelligence source was his engineers, because one of the key roles of the engineers in this era, much more so than today, was reconnaissance. Indeed, Weigley asserts that "Scott never sent troops to the attack without a full report on the approaches from the engineers" (*History* 185).

The reconnaissance efforts of young officers such as Lee, Beauregard, Zealous Tower, John Smith, and Joe Johnston were instrumental in allowing Scott to find routes that would allow him to turn the enemy and avoid costly frontal assaults. Nonetheless, the demands on the engineers were monumental. At Cerro Gordo, Lee had to hide behind a log while Mexican soldiers loitered nearby for a seeming eternity (Freeman, *Lee* 1:240–241). Douglas Southall Freeman describes the physical labor Lee expended at the Pedregal, writing that "Lee doubtless sought repose as soon as he could get it after the close of the battle. He had been on his feet or in the saddle almost continuously for thirty-six hours, had thrice crossed the pedregal [*sic*], and had been in all three of the actions, that of the 19th in the pedregal, that of Padierna, and that of Churubusco" (*Lee* 1:270–271).

Intelligence collection in this manner was largely a function of the skill of individual engineers. Upon returning from a reconnaissance, the engineer would brief the commander on his findings and actively participate in the ensuing discussion of the proposed plan of attack. It was a very personal system that was excessively dependent on a single source.

This weakness of being unable to collect, analyze, and disseminate information from a variety of sources would continue into the Civil War. Intelligence collectors would merely gather such varied sources as newspapers, reports from spies, balloon observations, and reports from runaway slaves and forward them to commanders without any real effort to analyze, deconflict, or put such information into context. The results were often widely exaggerated estimates, such as those that would plague McClellan during the Peninsula Campaign. It was not until Joe Hooker appointed Colonel George Sharpe as the head of the Bureau of Military Information that the Federal intelligence system began to take shape as a coordinated effort that provided commanders fairly reliable all-source intelligence.

While the Confederacy never produced an equivalent to Sharpe, it did have certain advantages in intelligence. The first was the great appreciation that Lee had gained for reconnaissance and the importance he attached to it. Second, there was a certain advantage the Confederacy had based on fighting on its own soil. Firsthand knowledge of the local terrain and access to a largely friendly population certainly helped Confederate intelligence efforts. Perhaps most important, however, certainly at the beginning of the war, was the superior Confederate cavalry. The cavalry would become the commander's eyes and ears in the Civil War, especially for Lee.

INFORMATION AND CAVALRY

Intelligence collection was not an uncharted role for the mounted forces. Ben McCulloch and his company of Texas Rangers had provided exactly such a service for Taylor in Mexico. In June 1846, McCulloch performed mounted reconnaissance for Taylor of a proposed route from Matamoros to Linares, and in February 1847 McCulloch's company and other cavalry under Charles May reconnoitered Agua Nueva and provided critical information about Santa Anna's whereabouts (J. Eisenhower, *So Far* 103–104, 181; Bauer 209).

It was in the Civil War, however, that the intelligence-gathering function of the cavalry accelerated. Here the Confederacy enjoyed a tremendous initial advantage, with Jeb Stuart providing valuable and timely reconnaissance for Lee. The Federal army had no counterpart equivalent to Stuart, and Federal commanders had great difficulty in determining the location and strength of Confederate forces. Stuart had a knack for interpreting what he saw on his rides and providing Lee with a perceptive intelligence summation. However, like many cavalry leaders, Stuart was vulnerable to succumbing to the theatrical side of his rides and would be unavailable when Lee needed him at Gettysburg (Weigley, *History* 239). The incident illustrates just how much commanders, especially Lee, depended on their cavalry to be their eyes and ears.

INFORMATION AND STAFFS

As commanding general during the Mexican War, Scott had been required to perform the functions of a modern general staff almost single-handedly. He had to devise the various war plans and make recommendations concerning their various merits to the president. He had to make estimates of the men and supplies those plans would require and then work out the details of the resourcing and supervise the execution. When Scott finally had the Vera Cruz preparations in enough semblance of order that he could depart Washington and take to the field, he left only the president, the secretary of war, and some of the bureau chiefs behind to act as the headquarters of the army. Weigley concludes that with Scott's departure, "a one-man general staff gave way to none at all" (*History* 179).

While in Mexico, Scott relied on his "little cabinet" of West Pointers to act as a relatively efficient staff. Robert E. Lee served as staff engineer, with Major John Lind Smith acting as chief engineer. Colonel Ethan Allen Hitchcock was inspector general, and Captain Henry Lee Scott was assistant adjutant general. Still, however, Scott's staff relied primarily on personal competence and energy rather than on any formal organization or procedure. The personal influence of staff officers in other commands is also clear. Captain William Bliss was assigned as Taylor's assistant adjutant general to help offset Taylor's administrative inattention (Weigley, *History* 181), and Joe Hooker was assigned as Brigadier General Thomas Hamer's chief of staff to compensate for Hamer's shortcomings (Hebert 26).

Some improvements would be made by the time of the Civil War, but staff functions remained rudimentary by modern standards. In 1855, Scott established a "general staff" and a "staff corps." The general staff consisted of a chief of staff, aides, an assistant adjutant general, and an assistant inspector general. The staff corps included engineering, ordnance, quartermaster, subsistence, medical, pay, signal, provost marshal, and artillery. Similar staff representation existed down to the regimental level, and, for the most part, Federal and Confederate staffs were organized along similar lines.

The staff maintained a very personal connection to the commander. The chief of staff and aides-de-camp were considered personal staff and would often depart when the commander was reassigned. These positions were frequently filled by relatives or close friends. For example, George McClellan appointed his father-in-law as his chief of staff.

This personal nature of the chief of staff position meant that commanders used their chiefs in a variety of ways. Seldom, however, was the chief of staff used as the central, coordinating staff authority, as the position is understood in today's army. In fact, the inadequate use of the chief of staff was one of the critical shortcomings of Civil War staffs. Another important deficiency was the lack of any formal operations or intelligence staff. Staff liaison among various headquarters was also informal and spotty at best (Gabel, *Vicksburg* 8–9).

INFORMATION AND COMMUNICATIONS

Communications during the Mexican War were a continual source of problems, largely because of the time and distances involved. In some cases, military dispatches from the field traveled on the same ship with stories filed by newspaper reporters on the scene, resulting in New Orleans newspapers blazoning war headlines days before the government in Washington had any inkling what had happened (J. Eisenhower, *So Far* 86).

When Washington did figure out what was going on, the information was not always welcome. For example, President Polk did not learn until October 11, 1846, of Taylor's victory at Monterey and the subsequent surrender agreement on September 25. When he did, Polk was infuriated that Taylor had agreed to a truce, something Polk believed "violated [Taylor's] express orders" and cost a speedy end to the war. Polk ordered the armistice terminated in a letter that reached Taylor on November 2. The slow nature of such communications not only hampered command guidance and decision making but also fostered an assumption of intrigue and duplicity that might have been avoided if more direct communications had been possible (J. Eisenhower, *So Far* 147–149, 159–160).

The communication problem was partially offset in the Civil War by increased use of the telegraph, a development that offered both strategic and operational capabilities. It was supplemented by line-of-sight systems, which offered operational and some tactical capability, and couriers, who were primarily a tactical asset.

In the area of the telegraph, the Federals had a significant advantage. Because the South lacked the resources and factories to produce wire, the Confederacy had to rely on existing telegraph lines, which limited the telegraph's operational significance. The Federals, however, used the magneto-powered Beardslee device as a basis for field telegraph units that carried operators and equipment throughout the countryside. Operators could hook insulated wire into existing trunk lines to reach into the civilian telegraph network and extend communications from the battlefield to the rear areas.

Line-of-sight communications were based on Albert C. Myer's "wigwag system," which used five separate, numbered movements of a single flag to communicate messages. Myer went on to serve as the first chief of the Federal Signal Corps. One of Myer's assistants in the prewar testing of the wigwag system was E. P. Alexander, who went on to organize the Confederate Signal Corps. On balance, Federal and Confederate visual communications capabilities were roughly equal.

Couriers offered a viable means of tactical communications, but were not completely reliable. Mounted staff officers or detailed soldiers would deliver messages from one headquarters to another, but the couriers were subject to being killed or becoming captured, lost, or delayed, and the messages could be misinterpreted, ignored, or made irrelevant by subsequent developments. Such weaknesses in the courier system tended to compound other command errors and misjudgments (Gabel, *Vicksburg* 59–60).

IMPACT

Partly because the army fought so well in Mexico and partly because any changes in military policy might have upset the delicate sectional balance, little changed in the army between the end of the Mexican War and the eve of the Civil War (Weigley, *History* 189). In terms of maneuver, Jominian thought still predominated, and formations were still tightly packed in the Napoleonic order to facilitate a massed volley of fire. Whatever had been learned about turning movements in Mexico was still complicated by difficulties in command and control, and frontal attacks would remain a common and costly feature of the Civil War. One major change would occur in the area of transportation, and the railroad would transcend the steamboat as the critical long-distance mover of supplies and men in the Civil War.

While great changes occurred in the area of firepower, notably the rifle and minié ball, Civil War commanders would be slow to recognize this dramatic development. The change, however, would be undeniable, and one of its effects would be a relegation of artillery to a predominantly defensive role in the Civil War.

Leadership, that quintessential element of war, would remain a mixed bag, ranging from political generals to consummate professionals. The small numbers involved in Mexico would come nowhere near the large armies of the Civil War, and span of control would be complicated by both the size of the armies and the quality of the leaders. The limited nature of the objectives in Mexico would also present a leadership challenge to those facing a more total-war scenario in the Civil War. Significantly, though, the West Pointers who proved so stellar as junior officers in Mexico would come of age as the senior leadership of the Civil War, and, as in Mexico, these officers would lead largely volunteer soldiers.

The new technology would profoundly affect protection in the Civil War. Those who had learned the dominance of the offensive in Mexico would have to come to grips with the increased strength of the defensive in the Civil War. Breastworks would take on a new significance, and engineering would be a major part of battlefield preparation. The vulnerability of logistics would continue to be a problem, and Civil War commanders would often resort to the Mexican War solution of living off the land. Fortunately, medical care and field sanitation would greatly improve, but the still limited knowledge of medicine and disease would continue to make war deadly.

The information available to commanders would improve, both by modest improvements in staffs and greater use of the cavalry, but a lack of intelligence would continue to plague decision making. The telegraph provided much greater connectivity at the strategic level, but true tactical-level communications would have to wait for the advent of the radio.

All in all, the American military system remained relatively unchanged, so that on the eve of the Civil War the experience from Mexico was still highly relevant and telling. Veterans of Mexico brought their experiences with them, and these experiences shaped their tactics, attitudes, decisions, and conduct in the Civil War. It is almost impossible to completely understand the leadership of the Civil War without first understanding its Mexican War proving ground.

PART ONE

THE FEDERALS

George McClellan
and Siege Warfare

As a young lieutenant in Mexico, George McClellan would have two formative experiences. First, he would witness Winfield Scott's magnificent amphibious turning movement and successful siege of Vera Cruz. McClellan would replicate this maneuver as commander of the Army of the Potomac during the Peninsula Campaign. Unfortunately for McClellan, his siege of Yorktown would not have the positive results Scott enjoyed in Mexico. Second, McClellan would observe what he considered the political mistreatment of Scott by President James Polk. From this experience, McClellan would gain a contempt for politicians that would negatively affect his relations with President Abraham Lincoln during the Civil War.

VERA CRUZ

McClellan arrived in Mexico in October 1846, but his most important experience with regard to his later Civil War conduct would come in March 1847 at Vera Cruz, a 13,000-man amphibious turning movement masterminded by General Winfield Scott. McClellan and his company of engineers landed with the first wave of regulars outside of Vera Cruz on March 9. The Mexicans failed to oppose the landing, and within four days the Americans had drawn their lines around the fortified city. Scott opted against a frontal assault and instead initiated a formal siege. The original siege train proved to be inadequate, and Scott arranged to borrow heavier ordnance from the navy (S. Sears, *McClellan* 18–19). The shelling began on March 22, a truce was granted on

March 26, and on March 27 the Mexican garrison surrendered. It was all relatively quick and painless. It was a lesson McClellan would not forget.

After the war, McClellan returned to an assignment at West Point, but his most significant peacetime army experience began on April 11, 1855, when he departed as part of a three-man military commission appointed by Secretary of War Jefferson Davis to study the latest military developments in Europe and observe the war in Crimea firsthand. Upon arrival, the commission was thwarted in its attempts to visit Sevastopol during the siege itself, but was able to inspect the abandoned works after the siege was lifted. McClellan spent much of his time studying the logistical aspects of the siege, to include the transportation of the allied forces by sea (S. Sears, *McClellan* 48). When he returned to the United States, McClellan opened his report with a critical analysis of the siege at Sevastopol. This experience built upon what McClellan had been a part of at Vera Cruz. Indeed, by this time no officer knew more about conducting a siege than did McClellan (S. Sears, *Gates* 39). This background would clearly influence McClellan's strategy and conduct on the Virginia Peninsula in the Civil War.

THE PENINSULA CAMPAIGN

Desiring to avoid the heavy, slow fighting of an overland campaign, McClellan, now commander of the Army of the Potomac, developed a plan to move from Alexandria, Virginia, by water to the peninsula between the James and York rivers and from there advance on Richmond. The movement began on March 17, 1862, and McClellan personally reached Fort Monroe on April 2. Opposing him was Major General John Magruder's Army of the Peninsula. Reports of Magruder's strength vary slightly, from Magruder's own reports of 11,000 or 11,500 to Stephen Sears's figures of 13,600 (S. Sears, *Gates* 26). Regardless of these discrepancies, what is certain is that when McClellan disembarked on April 2, he had 58,000 men compared to Magruder's much lower strength (Nevins 6:56). When McClellan actually began his march to Yorktown on April 4, he had about 70,000 men (T. Williams, *Lincoln* 88), although Clifford Dowdey believes barely 60,000 "were ready to move" (*Seven Days* 43). McClellan himself reports that he had "53,000 men in condition to move"

(McClellan 161). Even allowing for McClellan's lower figure, clearly at this juncture the amphibious move had presented the Federals with a very advantageous situation.

After failing to coordinate anything more ambitious with the navy, McClellan launched a very uncomplicated maneuver in which one column marched up the Peninsula on the right toward Yorktown while another marched on the left toward Williamsburg (Nevins 2:56). This left column was commanded by Brigadier General Erasmus Keyes. Late in the afternoon of April 5, Keyes's advance element came under fire from artillery and entrenched infantry at Lee's Mill, where the maps indicated only a harmless depot. At dusk, Keyes's force collapsed in an unorganized halt among the wooded swamps east of the Warwick. Based on this contact, Keyes reported that "Magruder is in a strongly fortified position behind Warwick River, the fords to which had been destroyed by dams, and the approaches to which are through dense forests, swamps, and marshes. No part of his line as far as discovered can be taken by assault without an enormous waste of life" (Nevins 2:56). Of course, such a brief contest could not have possibly warranted such a dramatic conclusion on Keyes's part. Had Keyes and the other Federal commanders probed a little more aggressively, they would have found that Magruder was in fact stretched quite thin (T. Williams, *Lincoln* 90).

Certainly for the first six or seven days of the operation, McClellan enjoyed a four to one numerical superiority over the Confederates (Nevins 6:58; Dowdey, *Seven Days* 46). In spite of this advantage, late on April 5 McClellan elected to begin preparations for a siege, even writing his wife to request she send him his books on Sevastopol (S. Sears, *Gates* 48). A British observer who had described the Army of the Potomac's first move in the campaign as "the stride of a giant" would pronounce the second step as "that of a dwarf" (S. Sears, *Gates* 39).

After the war, McClellan explained his decision, writing that he was "obliged to resort to siege operations in order to silence the enemy's artillery fire, and open the way to an assault" (163). In fact, Magruder's artillery posed only an imagined and exaggerated threat to McClellan. Bruce Catton concludes that McClellan "could certainly have overwhelmed Magruder with one push, and even after [overall Confederate commander General Joseph] Johnston got the rest of his army to the scene the Confederate works could probably have been stormed" (Catton, *Civil War* 64). Indeed, as Johnston reported on April 22, "No one but McClellan could have hesitated to attack" (Freeman, *Lee's Lieutenants* 1:154).

Instead of being genuinely concerned about the strength of Magruder's artillery, McClellan made the siege decision because that had been the course he had favored all along. The underdeveloped reports of Keyes merely gave him the excuse he needed to put the plan in motion. Brigadier General W. F. Barry, McClellan's chief of artillery, remembers the siege decision thusly: "The army having arrived in front of the enemy's works went into camp, and preparations were at once commenced on the siege. From this date until April 10 active reconnaissance of the enemy's lines and works were pushed by the commanding general . . . for the purpose of selecting a suitable place for the landing of the siege train" (Dowdey, *Seven Days* 46). Obviously, from the time of the initial contact with the enemy, McClellan had very little interest in engaging in a battle of maneuver.

Instead, McClellan's decision was based on his predilection for siege, with all its slow, deliberate execution and its small loss of life (T. Williams, *Lincoln* 90). These were the lessons McClellan had learned at Vera Cruz and Sevastopol. In fact, there is much to suggest that McClellan departed Washington with the idea of a siege already fixed in his mind (Nevins 6:58). Evidence of this intention can be found in the composition of McClellan's siege train, only half of which was regular siege guns. The other half was made up of seacoast guns weighing up to eight tons. These could not be moved at all in the field and had to be fired from stationary platforms. Such monsters could not be employed in a battle of maneuver against Magruder's Warwick River line (Dowdey, *Seven Days* 51), but they were the very type of heavier guns that McClellan saw Scott originally lacked at Vera Cruz. McClellan came ready for a siege.

The siege lasted until May 3, when the Confederates abandoned Yorktown and withdrew up the Peninsula on their own terms. By that time, Lee had affected the reconcentration of forces that would allow him ultimately to go on the offensive. Johnston gives great credit to Magruder for this turn of events, writing that Magruder's "resolute and judicious course . . . saved Richmond, and gave the Confederate Government time to swell that officer's handful to an army" (Stiles 25). In fact, the real credit for this opportunity lay with McClellan more than it did with Magruder. Due to his overcaution,

Thirteen-inch seacoast mortars used in the siege of Yorktown. Library of Congress, Prints and Photographs Division, reproduction number LC-B8171-0380 DLC (b&w film copy neg.).

McClellan lost the tremendous advantage he had gained in early April as the result of his amphibious move. In trying to replicate what he had learned from Scott at Vera Cruz, McClellan had failed on the Peninsula.

POLITICAL IMPLICATIONS

From the Mexican War, McClellan had also developed a thorough contempt for the civilian management of the war, and this became embedded in his military thinking (S. Sears, *McClellan* 25). Part of McClellan's opinion was surely influenced by his having to serve in Mexico under the politically appointed and largely incompetent Brigadier General Gideon Pillow and Major General Robert Patterson. An additional factor was what McClellan considered to be

President Polk's politically motivated relief of Scott in 1848. These misgivings would also shape McClellan's conduct during the Civil War.

Perhaps McClellan's greatest flaw regarding the Peninsula Campaign was his failure to adhere to the principle of war of objective, and McClellan's most serious failing here had to do primarily in the political rather than the military context. McClellan simply could not reconcile, let alone subordinate, his objectives to President Lincoln's.

In *On War*, Carl von Clausewitz wrote that "no major proposal required for war can be worked out in ignorance of political factors" (608), but McClellan's actions ignored this requirement. Herman Hattaway and Archer Jones observe that McClellan "seemed unable to grasp the political realities faced by an administration which sought to draw hostile elements into full support of the war for the Union" (98–99).

This represents what was one of McClellan's greatest shortcomings as Lincoln's subordinate—his failure to understand the president's developing grand strategy. Lincoln was considering options to expand the parameters of the war by drawing on a wide range of military, political, and economic weapons at his disposal. McClellan, due to his political beliefs and his deliberate nature, favored a much more restrictive and limited war. As Joseph Glatthaar observes, "Their opinions gravitated toward opposite poles" (81).

A large part of McClellan's political failure was his unabashed contempt for Lincoln and his failure to subordinate himself to civilian authority. T. Harry Williams contends that McClellan assumed "he was big enough to treat with the government as an equal party" (*Lincoln* 109). This attitude is perhaps best understood by a sampling of McClellan's comments on the government's leadership. He considered Lincoln to be "an idiot" and "nothing more than a well-meaning baboon." Secretary of State William Seward was a "meddling, officious, incompetent puppy." Secretary of the Navy Gideon Welles was "weaker than the most garrulous woman you were ever annoyed by." Attorney General Edward Bates was "an old fool." General in Chief Scott, McClellan's role model at Vera Cruz, was now "a perfect imbecile." Indeed, Glatthaar concludes that "anyone in the administration who crossed McClellan's path and did not yield wholeheartedly to his program came in for such epithets" (61). Sears agrees, writing that McClellan believed "anyone who did not support him in every aspect and without exception must be against him" (*Gates* 149).

A scenario completely unimaginable today illustrates the depth of McClellan's contempt and insubordination. One evening Lincoln, Seward, and presidential secretary John Hay dropped by McClellan's headquarters, only to learn that McClellan was at a wedding and would return shortly. McClellan did return in about an hour and upon being notified of his visitors, went upstairs anyway. After waiting another thirty minutes, Lincoln dispatched a servant to remind McClellan he was still downstairs. Moments later, the servant returned with a message that McClellan had gone to bed for the evening (Glatthaar 64). That Lincoln could maturely and selflessly overlook such a snub in deference to the greater emergencies of the time speaks as much about Lincoln's character as McClellan's egotistical behavior does about his.

McClellan had learned such contempt for civilian authority in Mexico. He now viewed himself to be the victim of Lincoln's incompetence and intrigue, as he had believed Scott was the victim of Polk's. Thus he considered Lincoln to be a meddling amateur, unworthy of his confidence or consultation, rather than his commander in chief. It was a fatal flaw that above all others made McClellan unsuited to command the Army of the Potomac, and it was a flaw whose first inklings can be traced to Mexico.

PREDICTABILITY

Ulysses Grant concluded that "McClellan is to me one of the mysteries of the war" (Young 264), and indeed McClellan is a psychoanalyst's dream. Theories are legion. Digging deep into McClellan's psyche, Ethan Rafuse attributes McClellan's caution and conservatism to his political background as a Whig (5). Peter Parish focuses on McClellan's personality, arguing that McClellan's

defects were his virtues carried to excess. His confidence became arrogance, or mere vanity. His thoroughness led him into over-caution, procrastination, and a perfectionism to which the hard and swiftly-changing realities of war could seldom conform. His flair for organization and planning betrayed him into inflexibility, a tendency to assume that the facts must inevitably fit his plans, and an inability to improvise or seize an unexpected opportunity. His military professionalism degenerated into a narrow exclusiveness, an ill-disguised contempt for his political masters, and a willful blindness to the non-military considerations which virtually affected grand strategy. His sense of mission caused him to see all who crossed him as conspirators and himself as a martyr. He had most of the talents, except the ability to put them to the greatest use. (192)

Yet certainly in Mexico McClellan had experiences that would reinforce the political background that Rafuse notes and would easily grow into the defects that Parish observes. From Vera Cruz, McClellan should have learned that siege warfare could be successful under certain circumstances. He did not learn, however, what those circumstances were, and he tried to apply the siege at Yorktown when the situation required something else. McClellan chose to remember only Scott's deliberate siege rather than his audacious march inland from Vera Cruz. McClellan's experience in Mexico imbued him with a cautious, inflexible approach to warfare that would not serve him well on the Peninsula, where, as Scott had advanced boldly to Mexico City, McClellan should have pressed on toward Richmond.

Likewise, the caution McClellan learned in Mexico about the political aspect of war grew into a defect in the Civil War. His suspicion of Lincoln prevented McClellan from adhering to the principle of war of objective, and he never synchronized his military actions with Lincoln's overall strategy. Again, McClellan's Mexican War experience, instead of creating a positive learning experience, created a defect. A more astute student than McClellan should have learned that the political aspect of war requires more communication between the commander and the president, not less. At a very minimum, McClellan should have learned, at Scott's expense, that presidential power is tremendous and must be treated with respect. Instead, McClellan learned to treat it with contempt. McClellan was exposed to some potentially valuable experiences in Mexico. Sadly for the Union cause, his personality turned them into negative lessons.

Ulysses S. Grant and Logistical Risk

William McFeely writes that though "[v]irtually unnoticed himself in the Mexican War, [Ulysses S.] Grant watched his fellow warriors carefully" (37). During the war, Grant served as the quartermaster and commissary of the Fourth Infantry Regiment. Grant bitterly opposed the posting because he feared it would rob him of combat experience, but it ultimately proved to be very fortuitous. Jean Edward Smith explains that in Mexico, Grant learned

> the intricacies of military logistics from the bottom up. For a man who would go on to command large armies, no training could have been more valuable. During the Civil War, Grant's armies might occasionally have straggled, discipline might sometimes have been lax, but food and ammunition trains were always expertly handled. While Grant's military fame deservedly rests on his battlefield victories, those victories depended on his skill as a quartermaster. Unlike many Union armies, the forces he led never wanted the tools of war. (52–53)

Much of Grant's quartermaster experience in Mexico dealt with routine issues of supply, but he also observed the audacious and spectacular interface of maneuver and logistics in General Winfield Scott's decision to operate independent of a fixed and fortified line of supply. It was a maneuver Grant himself would repeat during the Vicksburg Campaign in the Civil War.

SCOTT IN MEXICO

After a series of victories such as Vera Cruz and Cerro Gordo, Scott arrived in Puebla on May 28, 1847. John Eisenhower observes that at this juncture, Scott's "greatest practical problem was the maintenance of his communications with the coast" (*So Far* 297–298). Scott's supply line back to Vera Cruz was becoming increasingly costly to maintain. The problem was protecting his rear from Mexican guerrillas. In order to do this, Scott had been forced to leave garrisons at Vera Cruz, Jalapa, and Perote. This requirement, as well as other factors, had reduced Scott's active army at Puebla by 5,820 men. To regain strength, Scott ordered that all stations between Vera Cruz and Puebla would be abandoned. He was effectively cutting his army off from the coast. He would have no supply line. He would live off the land.

Scott's move was bold and audacious. It was also not without its critics. Upon learning of Scott's decision, the Duke of Wellington, who had been closely following the campaign, declared, "Scott is lost! He has been carried away by success! He can't take [Mexico City], and he can't fall back on his base" (J. Eisenhower, *So Far* 298).

Scott, however, would prove the skeptics wrong. He developed an effective system of local supply, which included the prohibition against forced requisition and the insistence upon the purchase of supplies (Weigley, *American Way* 72). By ridding himself of the requirement to secure his lines of communication with garrisons, Scott amassed an army of some 14,000 men (J. Eisenhower, *So Far* 306–307). Both this greater strength and his freedom from a fixed line of supply allowed Scott to fight the war of maneuver that he desired.

Scott's lead elements departed Puebla on August 7, 1847. By August 18, it appeared that the Duke of Wellington might be right after all. Scott's situation was by now serious if not desperate. Colonel Ethan Hitchcock wrote, "We have no forage for our horses; our hard bread is getting musty; we have four days' rations for the army and some beef on hoof." Kirby Smith wrote, "Mexico must fall or we must all find a grave between this and the city." Scott's bold move of cutting loose from his line of supply would require a quick victory to eliminate the danger to his army (J. Eisenhower, *Agent* 277).

Scott accomplished this requirement at Contreras and Churubusco on August 20. With these two victories, Scott had crossed the entire Valley of

Mexico. Russell Weigley observes, "Scott was a bold strategist. His march from Veracruz into the interior was one of the most daring movements of American military history" (*American Way* 75). Even the Duke of Wellington reversed himself, declaring Scott to be "the greatest living soldier" and urging young English officers to study the campaign as one "unsurpassed in military annals" (Millett and Maslowski 149).

GRANT AT VICKSBURG

As a young lieutenant, Ulysses Grant was a participant in this great campaign. He had done his share of fighting, but Charles Bracelen Flood highlights that in Mexico, Grant "had not only learned battlefield tactics . . . but, fully as important, had mastered his regiments complicated problems of supply and transportation" (18). Few problems could be more complicated than relying on the countryside as the primary source of sustenance. Serving as a quartermaster and commissary attached to Brigadier General William Worth's division, Grant describes in his *Memoirs* at least one instance in which he marched with a large wagon train to procure forage (66). The Mexican War had taught Grant that an army could reduce its line of supply and survive.

It was a lesson that Grant, now no longer a lieutenant but a major general in the Federal army, remembered in his Vicksburg Campaign during the Civil War. Grant's line of supply for his advance into Mississippi was the Mississippi Central Railroad, originating in Grand Junction, Tennessee. Maintaining the railroad cost the Federal army troops both to guard and repair it (Donovan et al. 103). It was the same problem Scott had faced in Mexico.

On December 12, 1862, Lieutenant General John Pemberton, the Confederate commander opposing Grant, ordered Major General Earl Van Dorn to take command of all the cavalry in the vicinity of Grenada, Mississippi; launch a sweep around Grant's left flank; destroy the Federal depot at Holly Springs; and wreck as much of the Mississippi Central and the parallel Memphis and Charleston Railroad as he could (Donovan et al. 141). On December 18, Van Dorn and 3,500 cavalrymen left Grenada, and on December 20 they surprised the weaker Federal force at Holly Springs, destroying an estimated half a million dollars worth of supplies there. From there, Van Dorn proceeded north, destroying as much of the railroad as he could before returning to Grenada on December 28 (Donovan et al. 106–107).

Simultaneously, a twin raid was conducted by Lieutenant General Nathan Bedford Forrest against the important rail junction at Jackson, Tennessee, on December 20 (Donovan et al. 106). The two raids left Grant in serious danger. Timothy Donovan writes, "To attempt to measure the amount of influence of the two cavalry raids on the subsequent decision by Grant to abandon his over-land approach can only lead to a subjective estimate at best. . . . [Nonetheless], the raids of Van Dorn and Forrest displayed cavalry in a classic example of the excellent use of a small, highly mobile unit in an economy of force role" (Donovan et al. 141–142). Indeed, the Confederate western commander Joe Johnston came to place his main effort for defeating Grant on cavalry raids against the vulnerable rail communications in western Tennessee (Hattaway and Jones 391–392). The Confederate raiders presented Grant with the same problem of a vulnerable line of supply as the Mexican guerrillas had presented Scott.

On May 3, Grant learned that Major General Nathaniel Banks would be delayed in joining him. In his *Memoirs*, Grant writes, "Up to this time my in-tention had been to secure Grand Gulf, as a base of supplies, detach [John] McClernand's corps to Banks and cooperate with him in the reduction of Port Hudson." With this new development, Grant instead "determined to move in-dependently of Banks, cut loose from my base, destroy the rebel force in rear of Vicksburg or invest or capture the city" (Grant 258). In implementing this decision, Grant drew heavily on his experience in Mexico. His leadership was detailed, involved, and expert. Jean Edward Smith states that "for the next four days Grant acted as the quartermaster he had been in the Mexican War, fir-ing off logistical instructions to subordinates, stockpiling ammunition, and dis-patching foraging parties into the countryside" (243).

Nonetheless, Grant certainly overstates the idea that he "cut loose" from his supply lines. As he moved east of the Mississippi, Grant continued to re-ceive a steady stream of supplies carried in wagons from Young's Point to Bow-er's Landing, where the supplies were loaded on steamboats and carried to Grand Gulf. From Grand Gulf, huge wagon trains, sometimes numbering up to 200 vehicles, then brought the supplies forward. What Grant did not do though was occupy and garrison his supply route, and this is where, like Scott, he assumed risk (Bearss 2:480–481; Arnold 127; Gabel, *Vicksburg* 49–50; Ballard, *Vicksburg* 92, 248).

While Grant still received supplies by wagons, he was clearly also drawing from the Confederate countryside. Even many of his wagons were brought in by scavenger teams. The result was "an abundant array of farm vehicles, ranging from long-tongued wagons designed for hauling cotton bales, to elegant plantation carriages, upholstered phaetons, and surreys. The vehicles were drawn by an equally odd assortment of horses, mules, and oxen—probably the most unmilitary military train ever assembled." The system worked. One of Grant's privates bragged, "We live fat" (J. Smith 243).

POINTS IN COMMON

Grant's decision regarding his logistics shared several things in common with Scott's in Mexico. First, it was daring and subject to criticism. Recognizing this, Grant purposely delayed notifying General in Chief Henry Halleck until it was too late to stop it because "I knew well that Halleck's caution would lead him to disprove of this course." Even Grant's friend William Sherman wrote Grant to advise him "of the impossibility of supplying our army over a single road" (Grant 258).

The second point of commonality is that both operations would involve forage. To Sherman's protestations, Grant replied, "I do not calculate upon the possibility of supplying the army with full rations from Grand Gulf. I know it will be impossible without constructing additional roads. What I do expect is to get up what rations of hard bread, coffee, and salt we can, and make the country furnish the balance" (Grant 258–259). Grant eventually got an efficient system of wagons rolling, but until then forage would tide his army over (Ballard, *Vicksburg* 257). In his *Memoirs*, Grant writes, "We started from Bruinsburg with an average of about two days' rations, and received no more from our supplies for some days; abundance was found in the meantime" (259). An Indiana soldier agreed, noting, "We live principally on the produce of the planter—think it excellent 'war policy' to quarter a hungry army on the produce of the enemy and on his own land" (Ballard, *Vicksburg* 248–249).

The third comparison is that time was critical. Even with the abundant forage Grant expected to find, he knew he could not afford any long halts at which local supplies would be exhausted. He would have to keep the army moving. To this end, he wrote Sherman, "It's unnecessary for me to remind you of the overwhelming importance of celerity in your movements" (Flood 161).

A fourth likeness is that Grant's decision also facilitated maneuver. Grant was able to position his army between Pemberton at Vicksburg and Johnston at Jackson. Through the use of interior lines, Grant now had the opportunity of "threatening both or striking at either" (Hattaway and Jones 392). So he did, capturing Jackson on May 14 and then defeating Pemberton at Champion's Hill on May 16. Pemberton then withdrew to Vicksburg, and on May 18 the siege began (Hattaway and Jones 392–394).

The final point, of course, is that both operations were successful. Weigley writes that Grant considered his decision to reduce his line of supply to be the most important innovation in the Vicksburg Campaign. While Pemberton was preoccupied with trying to cut Grant's reduced communications, Vicksburg fell to Grant's siege. While crediting Grant with a successful campaign, Weigley wryly adds, "Nevertheless, breaking away from the line of communication was not so much an innovation as Grant's accounts make it seem. Scott had essayed a similar gamble in Mexico" (*American Way* 140). Indeed, Grant had been there to observe it and no doubt learned and remembered the lesson.

We usually think of Grant as the Federal commander who eventually defeated the great Robert E. Lee in Virginia. His service as a quartermaster in Mexico is a footnote at best, but it was through that experience that Grant learned a valuable logistical lesson. Scott had shown him that under certain conditions, an army could accept risk with its line of supply, survive, and win. Putting his quartermaster experience to good effect, Grant replicated those conditions outside of Vicksburg in 1862–1863, but the impact did not stop there. Grant passed it on to his lieutenant, William Sherman, who used the same technique in his March to the Sea (Cleaves, *Thomas* 28).

Philip Kearny and
Reckless Courage

One of the most aggressive and combative officers in both the Mexican War and the Civil War was Philip Kearney. He certainly was not in the army because he had to be. Kearney had graduated from Columbia University in 1833 and later inherited a million dollars from his grandfather. Kearney was "a soldier for the love of soldiering" (Bill 15).

Prior to Mexico, Kearny had been sent to Europe to study European tactics and had actually served with the French army in Algiers in 1840. After Mexico, he resigned from the U.S. Army and again fought with the French in northern Italy. One French officer wrote that Kearny "went under fire as on parade with a smile on his lips." Winfield Scott would call Kearny "the bravest man I ever saw, and a perfect soldier" (Catton, *Lincoln's Army* 31). Indeed, Kearny loved a fight and was nothing if not brave.

THE GATES OF MEXICO CITY

On August 20, 1847, Americans and Mexicans fought the twin battles of Contreras and Churubusco. The towns were but seven miles apart, and the battles were fought within a few hours of each other. Most of the troops involved at Churubusco had participated in one way or another at Contreras.

After Contreras, Santa Anna was forced to rally what troops could be saved back within the walls of Mexico City. In order for him to do so, he would have to keep open the bridge over the Rio Churubusco. This bridge was protected by two key defensive positions, which Santa Anna ordered held at all costs. Forming the backbone of the defense would be the infamous San Patrico Battalion, American deserters who knew that capture meant death and who would fight accordingly.

In his haste to pursue the enemy, Winfield Scott unwisely failed to conduct reconnaissance and did not know the strength of the Mexican defenses. Instead, he ordered an all-out, headlong attack (J. Eisenhower, *So Far* 318–325). By brute force alone, the assault reduced the Mexican defenses and sent the enemy in flight.

The pursuit fell to Colonel William Harney's First Dragoons, one of the squadrons of which was commanded by Captain Kearny. When it became apparent to Harney that he would not be able to envelop the Mexicans, he ordered a halt, but Kearny pressed on. In this case it appears that Kearny failed to hear the command, but the event had been foreshadowed. While serving in Algiers with the French, Kearny's commander's orders had been "Charge, and when you hear the recall sounded, remember it is not for you" (Bill 15).

Kearny and Lieutenant Richard Ewell continued the pursuit all the way to the gates of Mexico City. Here they encountered heavy Mexican musket fire. Kearny ordered his men to dismount and carry the works. Unfortunately for Kearny, those in the rear of the charge had heard Harney's order and were retreating (Henry, *Mexican War* 281). Kearny found himself left with just two squads (Bill 281). The American pursuit was repulsed. Ulysses Grant wrote that Kearny "rode with a squadron of cavalry to the very gates of the city, and would no doubt have entered with his little force" had he not been wounded (71). Indeed, Kearny's left arm was so mangled in the battle that it would require amputation. In another instance of foreshadowing, Kearny had once remarked that he would give an arm to lead a cavalry charge. He got his wish—at the exact price offered (Catton, *Lincoln's Army* 31).

IN THE SADDLE AGAIN

At the outbreak of the Civil War, Kearny was appointed brigadier general, U.S. Volunteers, on May 17, 1861, and took command of the first New Jersey brigade to be formed. In this capacity, Kearny embarked with Major General George McClellan on the Peninsula Campaign. Kearny distinguished himself during the campaign but chafed under McClellan's cautious approach to war, deriding his commander as the "Virginia creeper" and declaring him "a dirty, sneaking traitor" (Bailey 129).

Shortly before Williamsburg, Kearny was promoted to command a division of the III Corps. The Confederates had withdrawn up the Peninsula from Yorktown, and Major General James Longstreet was covering their withdrawal from a light line of defenses around Williamsburg. Brigadier General Edwin Sumner was in charge of the Federal pursuit. To deal with the Confederates at Williamsburg, Sumner inexplicably ignored nearly 30,000 troops he had more readily available and ordered up Kearny's division, which had been the last to leave Yorktown. Sumner asked Kearny if he thought he could dislodge the Confederates, to which Kearny replied, "I can make my men follow me into hell!" (Harris 45).

With the same vigorous leadership he had shown in Mexico, Kearny pushed his men past the road jams of thousands of Federal soldiers, threatening to burn their baggage trains if they did not clear the road. His men threw off their knapsacks to speed their march.

When Kearny reached the front, he led the reconnaissance himself—clenching his horse's reins between his teeth and waving his saber with his good right arm. Kearny charged into the thick of the fighting, deliberately drawing fire to expose the Confederate positions.

Once he had determined the enemy strength, Kearny launched the attack. When some of the men hesitated, he shouted, "Don't flinch boys! They're shooting at me, not you." Kearny personally led the charge of the Second Michigan Infantry that retook some previously captured Federal artillery (Bailey 110–111).

Kearny's success was short-lived, and the Confederates proved able to continue to trade space for time in their withdrawal toward Richmond. Indeed, historians have criticized Kearny's rashness. Shawn Harris writes that "Kearny had retaken some of the ground [Joseph] Hooker had lost in the morning, but at the cost of decimating several of his regiments. . . . [A]ll that Hooker and Kearny had accomplished was the needless slaughter of their own men for a piece of ground the Confederates could not have cared less about" (46).

Harris's conclusions not withstanding, Kearny emerged from the Peninsula Campaign rivaled in popularity with the troops only by McClellan. One general was renowned for being overly zealous, the other for being overly cautious.

LUCK RUNS OUT

McClellan's Peninsula Campaign failed, and in spite of a victory at Malvern Hill, he decided to withdraw from the Peninsula. Kearny was livid, stating, "I, Philip Kearny, an old soldier, enter my solemn protest against this order to retreat. We ought instead of retreating to follow up the enemy and take Richmond. And in full view of all the responsibility of such a declaration, I say to you all, such an order can only be prompted by cowardice or treason" (Catton, *Lincoln's Army* 146). President Lincoln had also grown frustrated with McClellan and placed John Pope in field command of the Army of the Potomac. The change was small consolation for Kearny, who cared little more for Pope than he did McClellan (Catton, *Lincoln's Army* 31).

Pope proved not to be the answer to the Federal command problems. In the battle of Second Manassas, Robert E. Lee and Stonewall Jackson brilliantly combined to deal Pope a humiliating defeat. Kearny fought with his characteristic vigor, crashing into A. P. Hill at the left end of Jackson's line, initially bending it back and forcing Hill to call for reinforcements, but ultimately having to pull back.

Thus it was with the entire Army of the Potomac. On September 1, Pope was in full retreat from Centreville to Fairfax Court House. Lee had ordered Jackson to cross Bull Run to the north and swing around Centreville to cut Pope's line of retreat. South of Little River Turnpike, near an old mansion named Chantilly, the Federal IX Corps ran into Jackson. The Federals charged and at first broke the Confederate line. The Confederates regrouped, countercharged, and closed the gap.

Amid this stalemate, Kearny found men of the Twenty-first Massachusetts behind a fence at the edge of a cornfield. Kearny was in "an ungovernable rage" and without reconnaissance pronounced the field free of Confederates and ordered the regiment to advance. When an officer produced two captured Georgians as evidence of a Confederate presence in the cornfield, Kearny bellowed, "Damn you and your prisoners!" and spurred his horse into the field (Time-Life 166–167).

Rain was falling in torrents when Kearny came upon a shadowy group of soldiers and demanded, "What troops are these?" When the reply came back "Forty-ninth Georgia," Kearny wheeled his horse to flee, hanging over the side of his saddle Indian-style (Time-Life 166–167). He could not escape. A bullet struck his spine and traversed to his chest, killing him instantly.

The Confederates took Kearny's dead body to a farmhouse and laid it out with care. A. P. Hill came to pay his respects and lamented, "Poor Kearny! He deserved a better death than that" (Time-Life 166–167).

It was almost exactly fifteen years since Churubusco when Kearny and Ewell had charged the gates of Mexico City. Now Kearny was dead. Just a few days earlier, on August 29, Kearny's old Mexico comrade Richard Ewell had lost his leg fighting for the Confederacy at nearby Groveton (J. Eisenhower, *So Far* 326).

Issues of communications and span of control demanded that leadership in both Mexico and the Civil War be direct and personal. Obviously, there were risks associated with such a style of command. Kearney illustrates how leaders in both wars accepted and paid for such risks.

Samuel Du Pont and
the Naval Blockade

An early part of the U.S. strategy in the Mexican War was to blockade ports on Mexico's Gulf and Pacific coasts to prevent arms and ammunition from entering the country from Europe (Carney, *Gateway* 9). Accordingly, in July and August 1846 John Drake Sloat and Robert Stockton, successive commanders of the Pacific Squadron, established control of the Pacific coast from San Francisco to San Diego. On August 19, Stockton ordered Joseph Hull to blockade Mazatlan and Samuel Du Pont to blockade San Blas, about 125 miles south of Mazatlan. Stockton's aim was to seize Acapulco, about 500 miles south of Mazatlan, and use it in support of a joint army-navy expedition into Mexico. Thus began Du Pont's experience with blockading, an experience he would repeat on a much larger scale in the Civil War.

THE FIRST BLOCKADE OF MEXICO

On September 2, Du Pont, commanding the *Cyane*, captured two Mexican vessels in the harbor of San Blas. He then sailed north to the pearl-fishing town of La Paz, seized nine small boats there, and secured a promise of neutrality from the governor of Baja California. Moving north some 150 miles to Loreto, Du Pont seized two schooners on October 1, and on October 7 he shelled Guaymas and burned a brig there. On November 13, Du Pont followed Hull to San Francisco to replenish his dwindling supplies (Bauer 344; Weddle, *Tragic Admiral* 27). The blockade was lifted.

The first blockade of Mexico's west coast had lasted about four weeks. Its ineffectiveness taught Du Pont two key lessons: a blockading force must have enough ships to adequately cover all ports, and blockading ships had to be sustained with supplies and maintenance facilities to enable them to remain on station for extended periods. Du Pont's biographer Kevin Weddle notes, "These experiences would serve [Du Pont] well during the Civil War" (*Tragic Admiral* 28). But first the navy would try again off California.

ANOTHER FAILURE

Orders for a second blockade were issued on December 24. Again, it would be an ineffective effort. As other ships left the blockade for resupplies at San Francisco, Du Pont was left by himself. To provide the friendly inhabitants of La Paz and San Jose del Cabo with some semblance of protection, Du Pont resorted to sailing the *Cyane* back and forth between San Jose and Mazatlan. This opened Mazatlan to commerce, breaking the blockade. Eventually, Du Pont sailed for Hawaii for resupply (Bauer 345; Amero).

These experiences showed Du Pont firsthand the practical difficulties of a blockade. Such an undertaking is very resource intensive in terms of both ships and supplies. To maintain the blockade, ships cannot abandon their positions to get supplies. Either the resupply points must be close enough to facilitate the blockade or additional ships must come in to replace the departing ones. Again, Du Pont would carry these lessons into the Civil War. Mexico had given him, according to Robert Selph Henry, "a foretaste, on a most limited scale, of the duty which [Du Pont] was later to undertake on a grand scale off the south Atlantic coast of the Confederate states" (*Mexican War* 210). Indeed, Du Pont was one of the few officers in the Federal navy who would bring blockading experience into the Civil War (Weddle, "Blockade").

THE CIVIL WAR BLOCKADE

On April 19, six days after Fort Sumter, President Lincoln issued a proclamation declaring the blockade of the Southern states from South Carolina to Texas. On the 27th, the blockade was extended to Virginia and North Carolina.

As in Mexico, the purpose of the blockade was to isolate the Confederacy from European trade. The terms of the proclamation were:

> Now therefore I, Abraham Lincoln, President of the United States . . . have further deemed it advisable to set on foot a blockade of the ports within the States aforesaid, in pursuance of the laws of the United States and of the Law of Nations in such case provided. For this purpose a competent force will be posted so as to prevent entrance and exit of vessels from the ports aforesaid. If, therefore, with a view to violate such blockade, a vessel shall approach or shall attempt to leave any of the said ports, she will be duly warned by the commander of one of the blockading vessels, who will endorse on her register the fact and date of such warning, and if the same vessel shall again attempt to enter or leave the blockaded port, she will be captured, and sent to the nearest convenient port for such proceedings against her, and her cargo as prize, as may he deemed advisable. (Basler 338–339)

Responsibility for the Federal blockade strategy rested with the Navy Board (also called the Blockade Board, the Strategy Board, and the Committee on Conference) (Reed 8), which was presided over by Captain Samuel Du Pont. Two days before Du Pont arrived in Washington to assume his duties on the board, he recalled his previous blockading experience in a letter to a friend: "During the Mexican War I had two hard years' work at it, with endless correspondence with naval and diplomatic functionaries, for I established the first blockade on the western coast." In spite of these personal credentials, Du Pont ran the Navy Board without stifling creative thought (Weddle, *Tragic Admiral* iii). He and his colleagues issued six primary and four supplemental reports on the status of the Confederate coast and how best to influence it. Their findings formed the basis for future naval and amphibious operations. In the process, Du Pont was able to apply what he had learned in Mexico: blockades were long, drawn-out affairs that were difficult to manage, coordinate, and maintain (Weddle, *Tragic Admiral* 30).

Du Pont and the board knew that a sustainable blockade would need not just coaling stations but also depots to store provisions and serve as refuges.

Much of the board's work involved not just determining blockade points but also determining which areas could be turned into bases for the fleet. Du Pont did not want a repeat of his Mexican War experience of having to lift the blockade to get resupplied.

As a result of this planning, the Federals experienced quick successes at Hatteras Inlet, South Carolina, and Ship Island, Mississippi. The target for the third operation would be Port Royal Sound, South Carolina. Neither the Hatteras Inlet nor the Ship Island operation had given the Federal fleet the large, deep-water harbor it needed in order to maintain a year-round blockade of key ports such as Wilmington, Charleston, and Savannah. Port Royal represented such a prize. It was the finest natural harbor on the Southern coast and would float the navies of the world (Weddle, *Tragic Admiral* 126–127; Foote 1:116). Furthermore, from Port Royal the Federals could also gain access to a series of inland waterways from which to blockade the coast from just below Charleston to the Saint Johns River in Florida without having to risk the uncertainties of the Atlantic. Du Pont's first blockade in Mexico had taken place during the hurricane season. He knew about the effects of weather. Under this plan, the Federals could block the neck of the bottle out of which the Confederate vessels had to emerge without having to be in the open sea themselves (Weigley, *American Way* 99).

PORT ROYAL

The Navy Board knew that the Port Royal operation would be its biggest effort to date. Success would require a strong force and the element of surprise. Thus the Navy Board would take no chances—Du Pont himself would head the expedition. He was promoted to flag officer and given command of the South Atlantic Blockading Squadron. Again, Mexico had prepared Du Pont for the rigors of independent command.

Du Pont's fleet would consist of 51 ships, 15 of which were warships, and a land force of almost 13,000 men (Weddle, *Tragic Admiral* 129). The warships given him were the navy's best, (Catton, *Hallowed* 85), and his fleet represented the largest assembled to date under the American flag (Rosengarten 213; Van Doren Stern 54).

On October 20, Du Pont and his fleet put out of Hampton Roads, Virginia, heading south. The hoped-for surprise did not last for long. That same day the Confederate government alerted its coastal defenses that the force had sailed. On November 1, Confederate secretary of war Judah Benjamin received intimation that the Federals were bound for Port Royal, and on November 4 the Port Royal defenders were telegraphed that "the enemy's expedition is intended for Port Royal" (Foote 1:117). Confederate president Jefferson Davis had for some time thought that the Southern coast needed additional defenses, and on November 6 he reorganized the coasts of South Carolina, Georgia, and north Florida into a single department and named General Robert E. Lee as its commander (Freeman, *Lee* 1:606; Foote 1:116–117; Dowdey and Manarin 81).

Du Pont had studied closely Flag Officer Silas Stringham's battle at Hatteras Inlet, as well as the battles at Odessa and Sevastopol during the Crimean War. In the Crimea, the ships had failed against the forts, but they had come close enough that, when considered along with Stringham's victory, Du Pont thought that the old dictum of the superiority of the fort over the ship might be broken. The key elements working to change the historic balance were the shell gun and the steam engine. Port Royal Sound was big enough to allow maneuver, and Du Pont planned to use his steam engines to keep his ships moving in an elliptical pattern, which would keep the two Confederate forts, Fort Walker and Fort Beauregard, under continuous fire. However, unlike Stringham, Du Pont would not be able to outrange the Confederate batteries (Weigley, *American Way* 99–100).

At 8:00 A.M. on November 7, the attack began. Du Pont had divided his force into a main squadron of nine of his heaviest frigates and sloops and a flanking squadron of five gunboats. With the *Wabash* in the lead, the Federals entered the sound in parallel columns and began receiving fire from the forts. Du Pont's plan was for the lighter squadron to operate on the right and pass midway between the two forts, both drawing and returning fire. It would also be ready to peel off and engage targets of opportunity, to include the Confederate ships, as they presented themselves. As this was unfolding, Commodore Joseph Tattnall brought his Confederate flotilla down the sound and engaged the *Wabash*. Du Pont's gunboats went after him, and Tattnall beat a hasty retreat three miles northwest of Fort Walker and took refuge at the mouth of Skull Creek. Dipping his pennant three times in a jaunty salute to his old

Fort Beauregard. Library of Congress, Prints and Photographs
Division, reproduction number LC-B8171-0203 DLC (b&w film neg.).

messmate, Tattnall was bottled up by the Federal gunboats and out of the
fight for good.

In the meantime, the main Federal squadron was executing its elliptical
pattern, advancing about two miles beyond the entrance of the sound on the
Fort Beauregard side and then turning left and returning on the Fort Walker
side. With each pass, the squadron widened its course so as to bring its guns
closer to the target. These constant changes in speed, range, and deflection
made the Federal fleet extremely hard for the Confederate gunners to engage
(Weddle, *Tragic Admiral* 132). With a bit of understatement, E. A. Pollard ad-
mits that "this manoeuvre doubtless disturbed the aim of the artillerists in the
forts" (194).

To make matters worse, the Confederate gunners had more problems than
just the moving targets. They were low on ammunition, and some of what they

had was the wrong size for their guns. Additionally, they had inferior powder and defective fuses (Weddle, *Tragic Admiral* 130; Foote 1:119; Chaitin 20). The Confederates were clearly at a disadvantage.

What had made this so, even more than the disparity in arms, was Du Pont's brilliant scheme of maneuver. Fort Walker had been built to defend against an attacking force moving straight in from the sea. Thus its northern flank was its weakest, a fact that Du Pont had learned from reconnaissance. Du Pont's plan took full advantage of this condition.

Confederate resistance did not last long. As Du Pont began his third ellipse, he received word that Fort Walker had been abandoned. At 2:20 P.M., a naval landing party raised the U.S. flag over the wreckage, and by nightfall army troops had landed and occupied the fort. Fort Beauregard, which was merely an adjunct to Fort Walker, lowered its flag at sunset, and early the next morning Federal troops crossed the water and occupied it as well. In the words of Shelby Foote, for the Confederates, "the fight had been lost from the moment Du Pont had conceived his plan of attack" (1:118–119).

The Federals lost eight killed and twenty-three wounded. The Confederates lost about 100 men. The victory gave the Federals an excellent harbor in both the sentimental heartland of secession and in an important cotton-producing region. Within three days, the Federals moved up the rivers and inlets and occupied the towns of Beaufort and Port Royal. The Federals now had an important foothold just fifty miles from Charleston (Weddle, *Tragic Admiral* 140; Foote 1:119–120; Pollard 194). By December, planters along the Georgia–South Carolina coast were burning cotton to prevent its capture (Thomas, *Confederate* 125).

THE IMPACT OF THE BLOCKADE

Historians differ over their conclusions about the effectiveness of the blockade, and certainly a variety of factors, of which the blockade was only one, defeated the Confederacy's economy. Yet as the Federals became more expert at blockading, the overall effect became noticeably more pronounced. Chances of capture while running the blockade in 1861 were estimated to be one in ten. By

1864, they were one in three. In 1860, the South was exporting $191,000,000 worth of cotton. By 1862, that had shrunk to $4,000,000 (Boatner 70). The blockade was only one reason for this, but as Allan Nevins writes, "it was perhaps the major element in garroting the South" in the end (8:272). Hard lessons that Samuel Du Pont learned blockading in Mexico and applied along the Confederate coast helped make this possible.

WINFIELD SCOTT
AND THE CHANGING
NATURE OF WARFARE

John Eisenhower identifies Winfield Scott as "the first truly professional soldier in the American military establishment," and credits Scott with being "the country's most prominent general" from 1821 to 1861 (*Agent* xiii). Scott's military exploits are truly amazing. Unfortunately, he is most commonly fixed in the popular imagination as the rotund and aged figure depicted in the famous 1861 Matthew Brady portrait. While this image does not do justice to Scott's lifetime of service, it does provide a hint to the fact that by the time of the Civil War, the nature of warfare had changed, leaving Scott behind.

TO MEXICO CITY

At the time of the Mexican War, Scott was at the zenith of his career. He had been a general for thirty-two years, and his service included the War of 1812, the Seminole War, several peaceable Indian removals, and diplomatic efforts on the northern frontier. He was in his fourth year as general in chief (J. Eisenhower, *Agent* 233). On November 19, 1846, President James Polk offered Scott command of an amphibious operation aimed at Vera Cruz. From there, Scott was to advance inland toward Mexico City.

For Scott, Mexico was a war of limited objectives, to be waged by limited means (T. Williams, *History* 178). Accordingly, his strategy would be largely a

General Winfield Scott. Matthew Brady Studio, Imperial salted-paper print, circa 1861, 47 x 39.9 cm (18 1/2 x 15 3/4 inches). National Portrait Gallery, Smithsonian Institution, Washington, D.C. Retrieved from NARA http://www.archives.gov/research_room/research_topics/civil_war/images/civil_war_174.jpg.

political one. He believed that Mexican political life centered around Mexico City so completely that capturing the capital would paralyze the country and oblige the Mexican government to sue for peace in order to remain a government. Thus his objective was to capture Mexico City, not to destroy the Mexican army (Weigley, *American Way* 74; T. Williams, *History* 178).

Such a strategy would also minimize casualties, both American and Mexican. Scott feared that costly battles would inflame Mexican emotions and therefore prolong the war. Therefore after his victories at Contreras and Churubusco, he agreed to an armistice rather than pressing his advantage and pursuing the fleeing Mexicans. Likewise Scott opted to preserve American lives by fighting a war of maneuver, seeking to flank his opponents rather than attack them frontally. Throughout the campaign, Scott conducted himself with strict regard for the rights of the Mexican civilian population. He imposed tight regulations on his own men, reduced opportunities for friction to the minimum, forbade forced requisitions, and insisted on purchasing supplies, all in spite of his precarious logistical situation. Once he reached Mexico City, he imposed a very lenient occupation without any of the harsh punishments of a conqueror. As Scott predicted, the country fell into paralysis, and the government sought a peace. Russell Weigley summarizes that Mexico allowed Scott "to wage limited war in the pre-Napoleonic, eighteenth-century style most congenial to him" (*American Way* 71–75).

ANACONDA

With the outbreak of the Civil War, Scott still enjoyed an amazing reputation. Eisenhower notes, "Winfield Scott was the man on whom all others in the Lincoln administration depended, the 'old soldier,' the repository of knowledge and understanding of military matters" (*Agent* 381). President Lincoln thus counted on Scott to produce a strategy.

As in Mexico, Scott sought to avoid a bloody war. To do so, he planned to mobilize an army so big and powerful that the Confederacy would negotiate a return to the Union without a fight. In the meantime, he envisioned seizing the entire line of the Mississippi and Ohio rivers in order to split the Confederate states east of the Mississippi from those in the west. At the same time, he would impose a naval blockade of the Confederate coast. By tightening this ring around the eastern Confederate states, large-scale fighting might be avoided. Scott argued that his plan "will thus cut off the luxuries to which the people are accustomed; and when they feel the pressure, not having been exasperated by attacks made on them within their respective States, the Union spirit will assert itself; those who are on the fence will descend on the Union side, and I will guarantee that in one year from this time all difficulties will be settled." If, on the other hand, Lincoln chose to invade the South, Scott predicted, "I will guarantee that at the end of a year you will be further from a settlement than you are now" (Doughty 115). The plan became known as the Anaconda Plan, because, like the big snake, it would squeeze the Confederacy (Doughty 115; J. Eisenhower, *Agent* 385–386).

Scott's plan was strategically sound, and by the end of the war, the Union had implemented it in full. However, it simply would not pass political muster in 1861. The public and the Lincoln administration had no stomach for such a time-consuming strategy. The cry then was for an immediate, all-out assault on the Confederate army, not a long, drawn-out strategy of exhaustion (J. Eisenhower, *Agent* 386–387). Scott's Anaconda Plan was rejected.

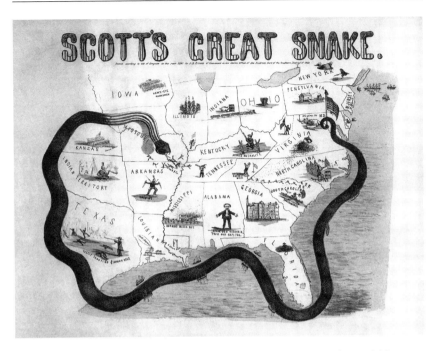

The Anaconda Plan: Scott's great snake. Library of Congress, Geography and Map Division, Washington, D.C., G3701.S5 1861 .E4 CW 11.

It was becomingly increasingly clear that Scott was being rejected as well. His belief, demonstrated in Mexico, that wars should be limited in objective and could be won without engaging in serious fighting did not suit the situation of the Civil War (T. Williams, *History* 250). Scott hung on for a little while, helping the nation recover from the defeat at First Manassas, but younger generals, namely George McClellan, were rising amid Scott's decline. On November 1, 1861, he retired from the army.

WHAT HAPPENED?

Scott had simply failed to keep up with the times. His military ideas were rooted in the classical military age of eighteenth-century Europe. Even as he presided over the mammoth gathering of the Civil War army of citizen soldiers, Scott felt most at home with a small professional army. Indeed, Allan Peskin attributes Scott's development of the Anaconda Plan not to "inappropriate lessons Scott had learned from his Mexican experience" but instead, in part at least, to his preference for regulars over volunteers. Peskin argues that in Mexico, Scott sought to "strike directly for the Mexican capital and end the war with one blow, a very different plan than the slow economic strangulation he advocated in 1861" (250). But Peskin misses the fact that both plans were steeped in limited-war theory. They were designed to avoid casualties, focused on geography rather than enemy armies, and aimed at political settlements. Ending the Mexican War "with one blow" would have meant destroying Santa Anna's army in a single decisive battle. Scott landed at Vera Cruz in March and did not enter Mexico City until September. Strategically, both in Mexico and the Civil War, Scott was at his best in a war of limited objectives, achievable by maneuver and occupation of territory rather than by ruthless destruction (Weigley, *American Way* 66).

Weigley describes Scott's passing from preeminence almost as one would describe a tragic hero. Weigley concludes that the Civil War would "suggest that while Scott was the preeminent military strategist of the first half of the nineteenth century, he occupied a lonely plateau in more senses than one: that at the zenith of his powers he was already a museum piece, a soldier of an age gone by whose perceptions of war and strategy had little influence on most of the very West Point graduates whose service in Mexico he so fulsomely praised, because the young graduates inhabited a new world of very different values from Scott's, the military world of Napoleon" (*American Way* 76).

John Pope and
the Influence of
Zachary Taylor

Besides Winfield Scott, the other major army commander in the Mexican War was Zachary Taylor. While Scott would march from his amphibious landing site at Vera Cruz inland to Mexico City, Taylor's campaign would lead him from Texas into northern Mexico. Scott was "Old Fuss and Feathers" while Taylor was "Old Rough and Ready." If Scott epitomized the incipient professionalism of the mid-nineteenth-century officer corps, Taylor was in many respects a throwback to the amateurishness of the War of 1812 (Doughty 83, 87). While Scott was refining the turning movement as the preferred form of maneuver, Taylor saw war as little more than marching and fighting (Jones 268), preferring to throw his troops against a strong enemy line rather than take the time to reconnoiter it (T. Williams, *History* 165)

In spite of, or perhaps because of, his informal and homespun manner, Taylor was very popular with the junior officers. Ulysses Grant was an officer who served under both Taylor and Scott, and perhaps patterned himself more after Taylor. Comparing the two, Grant wrote,

> I have now been in battle with the two leading commanders conducting armies in a foreign land. General Taylor never wore uniform, but dressed himself entirely for comfort. He moved about the field in which he was operating to see through his own eyes the situation. Often he would be without staff officers, and when he was accompanied by them there was no prescribed order in which they

followed. . . . General Scott was the reverse in all these particulars.
He always wore all the uniform prescribed or allowed by law when
he inspected his lines; word would be sent to all division and brigade commanders in advance, notifying them of the hour when the
commanding general might be expected. This was done so that all
the army might be under arms to salute their chief as he passed. On
these occasions he wore his dress uniform, cocked hat, aiguillettes,
sabre and spurs. His staff proper, besides all officers . . . followed,
also in uniform and in prescribed order. Orders were prepared with
great care and evidently with the view that they should be a history
of what followed.

In their modes of expressing thought, these two generals con-
trasted quite as strongly as in their other characteristics. General
Scott was precise in language, cultivated a style peculiarly his own;
was proud of his rhetoric; not averse to speaking of himself, often
in the third person, and he could bestow praise upon the person he
was talking about without the least embarrassment. Taylor was not a
conversationalist, but on paper he could put his meaning so plainly
that there could be no mistaking it. He knew how to express what
he wanted to say in the fewest well-chosen words, but would not
sacrifice meaning to the construction of high-sounding sentences.
But with their opposite characteristics both were great and successful soldiers; both were true, patriotic and upright in all their dealings. Both were pleasant to serve under—Taylor was pleasant to
serve with. Scott saw more through the eyes of his staff officers than
through his own. His plans were deliberately prepared, and fully expressed in orders. Taylor saw for himself, and gave orders to meet
the emergency without reference to how they would read in history.
(66–67)

Many officers such as Grant and Meade had the opportunity to serve
under both commanders when some 4,000 of Taylor's troops in northern
Mexico were diverted to support Scott's Vera Cruz operation. Such officers
were exposed to the two differing leadership styles. Others who served under
only Taylor did not benefit from Scott's more professional example. John Pope

was one of those who saw only one side of the American high command in Mexico. His attitude toward the rights of civilians and private property during the Civil War may reflect this experience.

THE TOPOGS

At the time of the Mexican War, two separate engineering corps existed in the U.S. Army. There was the Corps of Engineers, which counted among its members Robert E. Lee, P. G. T. Beauregard, Henry Halleck, and George McClellan, and there was the Corps of Topographical Engineers, which included George Meade, Joe Johnston, John C. Frémont, and John Pope. The topographical engineers, or "topogs," were responsible for topography, mapping, and civil engineering projects authorized by Congress such as roads, canals, railways, lighthouses, and public buildings and works. The Corps of Engineers was responsible for military engineering support to armies in the field and construction of fortifications (Traas 5–6).

John Pope served as a topog for General Taylor in Mexico. He received a brevet promotion to first lieutenant after Monterey, and after that battle he conducted a triangulation survey around the city (Traas 137). After Buena Vista, Pope became a brevet captain, helped complete a survey of the battlefield, and made a recon of the San Luis Potosi road to Cedral (Traas 144–145, 147). His entire service was under Taylor in the northern theater.

DIFFERENCES BETWEEN SCOTT AND TAYLOR

Scott preferred a limited approach to war. He was appalled by what he saw after a visit to Taylor's army, writing the secretary of war:

> But, my dear Sir, our militia & volunteers, if a tenth of what is said to be true, have committed atrocities—horrors—in Mexico, sufficient to make Heaven weep, & every American, of Christian morals, *blush* for his country. Murder, robbery & rape of mothers & daughters, in the presence of the tied up males of their families,

have been common all along the Rio Grande. . . . Truly it would
seem unchristian & cruel to let loose upon any people—even
savages—such unbridled persons—freebooters, &c., &c. (Weigley,
History 187–188)

Instead, Scott conducted his campaign with strict regard for the rights of
the Mexican citizens, making every effort to confine bloodshed and suffering to the Mexican army rather than the civilian population. He scrupulously
regulated his soldiers' conduct and interaction with Mexican civilians, reducing contact to the minimum necessary for the sustenance of his army and the
morale of his troops. In spite of his tenuous logistical situation, he prohibited forced requisitions and insisted upon the purchase of supplies (Weigley,
American Way 72).

Conversely, Taylor waged war with a much more wanton and destructive
style. He mismanaged his logistics and exercised relatively lax discipline in allowing his troops to plunder the Mexican countryside and its inhabitants in
order to make up the difference (Weigley, *American Way* 73).

In one example, a company of Texas Rangers occupied Reynosa as a forward base on the approach to Monterey during the Fourth of July holiday.
They celebrated by consuming two horse-troughs of whiskey as well as a large
number of local chickens and hogs that died "accidentally" during the festivi-
ties. Taylor did little to stop the outrageous conduct (Carney, *Gateway* 15).

Similarly, after Buena Vista, Taylor's main effort centered largely on anti-
guerrilla operations. Much of his soldiers' conduct in this campaign was of
dubious propriety. When a former member of the First Missouri Mounted
Riflemen was killed by guerrillas near Camargo, local authorities rounded up
several suspects, but then released them when they found there was insufficient evidence against them. On their way home, the group was ambushed by
some Americans, who killed four or five of the Mexicans. Taylor responded to
Mexican complaints of these murders and to allegations of rape, robbery, and
plunder by saying he did not condone the atrocities. Nonetheless, he took little
action to prevent them, blaming most of the problems on discharged volunteers returning home (Bauer 220–221).

But Taylor's efforts to put the blame elsewhere do not withstand scrutiny
when compared to other commanders in similar situations. K. Jack Bauer notes
the difference between Taylor's approach and John Wool's, writing:

Wool published an order reminding his command of the imperative of the practical necessity as well as the moral imperative of good treatment of the Mexican civilians. Wool strictly enforced the order despite the rough character of some of his men. This, together with Wool's insistence on scrupulous payment for goods taken, kept incidents to a minimum. It was a sharp contrast to the experience of Taylor's army and demonstrated the value of having a strict disciplinarian at the head of volunteer forces. (147)

Bauer acknowledges that "it would have been difficult for any commander of a force including significant numbers of poorly disciplined volunteers to prevent these collisions [between American soldiers and Mexican civilians], but other commanders, notably Wool and Scott, devised methods of holding incidents to a minimum" (102). In Mexico, Pope served exclusively, and perhaps to his detriment, in the environment of Taylor's command.

POPE'S GENERAL ORDERS

On June 26, 1862, Pope assumed command of the new Army of Virginia. He issued an abrasive and boastful address on July 14 that served to alienate and insult many in his new command and then issued a series of General Orders that certainly enraged the Confederacy and showed he had an aggressive and hostile policy toward civilians and private property beyond that of even Taylor in Mexico.

Four days after his initial address, Pope issued General Orders No. 5, stating that his army should live off the land:

GENERAL ORDERS NO. 5
HEADQUARTERS ARMY OF VIRGINIA
Washington, July 18, 1862

Hereafter, as far as practicable, the troops of this command will subsist upon the country in which their operations are carried on. In all cases supplies for this purpose will be taken by the officers to whose department they properly belong under the orders of the commanding officer of the troops for whose use they are intended. Vouchers will be given to the owners, stating on their face that they will be payable at the conclusion of the war, upon sufficient testimony being furnished that such owners have been loyal citizens of the United States since the date of the vouchers. Whenever it is known that supplies can be furnished in any district of the country where the troops are to operate the use of trains for carrying subsistence will be dispensed with as far as possible.

By command of Major-General Pope:
GEO. D. RUGGLES,
Colonel, Assistant Adjutant-General, and Chief of Staff.

(O. R., 12, part 2, 50)

This was supplemented by General Orders No. 7, which outlined how Pope planned to deal with the local citizenry. Pope's policy showed clear disregard for due process and suggests he approved of how Taylor's men summarily executed the suspected guerrillas near Camargo:

GENERAL ORDERS No. 7.
HEADQUARTERS ARMY OF VIRGINIA,
Washington, July 10 [?], 1862.

The people of the valley of the Shenandoah and throughout the region of operations of this army living along the lines of railroad and telegraph and along the routes of travel in rear of the United States forces are notified that they will be held responsible for any injury done to the track, line, or road, or for any attacks upon trains or straggling soldiers by bands of guerrillas in their neighborhood. No privileges and immunities of warfare apply to lawless bands of individuals not forming part of the organized forces of the enemy nor wearing the garb of soldiers, who, seeking and obtaining safety on pretext of being peaceful citizens, steal out in rear of the army, attack and murder straggling soldiers, molest trains of supplies, destroy railroads, telegraph lines, and bridges, and commit outrages disgraceful to civilized people and revolting to humanity. Evil-disposed persons in rear of our armies who do not themselves engage directly in these lawless acts encourage them by refusing to interfere or to give any information by which such acts can be prevented or the perpetrators punished.

Safety of life and property of all persons living in rear of our advancing armies depends upon the maintenance of peace and quiet among themselves and upon the unmolested movements through their midst of all pertaining to the military service. They are to understand distinctly that this security of travel is their only warrant of personal safety.

It is therefore ordered that wherever a railroad, wagon road, or telegraph is injured by parties of guerrillas the citizens living within 5 miles of the spot shall be turned out in mass to repair the damage, and shall, beside[s], pay to the United States in money or in property, to be levied by military force, the full amount of the pay and subsistence of the whole force necessary to coerce the performance of the work during the time occupied in completing it.

If a soldier or legitimate follower of the army be fired upon from any house the house shall be razed to the ground, and the inhabitants sent prisoners to the headquarters of this army. If such an outrage occur[s] at any place distant from settlements, the people within 5 miles around shall be held accountable and made to pay an indemnity sufficient for the case.

Any persons detected in such outrages, either during the act or at any time afterward, shall be shot, without awaiting civil process. No such acts can influence the result of this war, and they can only lead to heavy afflictions to the population to no purpose.

It is therefore enjoined upon all persons, both for the security of their property and the safety of their own persons, that they act vigorously and cordially together to prevent the perpetration of such outrages.

Whilst it is the wish of the general commanding this army that all peaceably disposed persons who remain at their homes and pursue their accustomed avocations shall be subjected to no improper burden of war, yet their own safety must of necessity depend upon the strict preservation of peace and order among themselves; and they are to understand that nothing will deter him from enforcing promptly and to the full extent every provision of this order.

By command of Major-General Pope:
GEO. D. RUGGLES,
Colonel, Assistant Adjutant-General, and Chief-of-Staff.

(O. R., 12, part 2, 51)

Pope went even further with General Orders No. 11, calling for the immediate arrest of all disloyal male citizens and compelling them either to take an oath of allegiance to the United States or be deported farther south:

GENERAL ORDERS No. 11.
HEADQUARTERS ARMY OF VIRGINIA,
Washington, July 23, 1862.

Commanders of army corps, divisions, brigades, and detached commands will proceed immediately to arrest all disloyal male citizens within their lines or within their reach in rear of their respective stations.

Such as are willing to take the oath of allegiance to the United States and will furnish sufficient security for its observance shall be permitted to remain at their homes and pursue in good faith their accustomed avocations. Those who refuse shall be conducted South beyond the extreme pickets of this army, and be notified that if found again anywhere within our lines or at any point in rear they will be considered spies, and subjected to the extreme rigor of military law.

If any person, having taken the oath of allegiance as above specified, be found to have violated it, he shall be shot, and his property seized and applied to the public use.

All communication with any person whatever living within the lines of the enemy is positively prohibited, except through the military authorities and in the manner specified by military law; and any person concerned in writing or in carrying letters or messages in any other way will be considered and treated as a spy within the lines of the United States Army.

By command of Major-General Pope:
GEO. D. RUGGLES,
Colonel, Assistant Adjutant-General, and Chief of Staff.

(O. R., 12, part 2, 52)

Pope appeared naively surprised when he learned that soldiers had taken his orders as a license to plunder and maraud, and on August 14 he attempted to correct this situation with General Orders No. 19:

GENERAL ORDERS No. 19.
HEADQUARTERS ARMY OF VIRGINIA,
Near Cedar Mountain, Va., August 14, 1862.

The major-general commanding discovers with great dissatisfaction that General Orders, No. 5, requiring that the troops of this command be subsisted on the country in which their operations are conducted, has either been entirely misinterpreted or grossly abused by many of the officers and soldiers of this command. It is to be distinctly understood that neither officer nor soldier has any right whatever, under the provisions of that order, to enter the house, molest the persons, or disturb the property of any citizen whatsoever.

Whenever it is necessary or convenient for the subsistence of the troops, provisions, forage, and such other articles as may be required will be taken possession of and used, but every seizure must be made solely by the order of the commanding officer of the troops then present and by the officer of the department through which the issues are made. Any officer or soldier who shall be found to have entered the house or molested the property of any citizen will be severely punished. Such acts of pillage and outrage are disgraceful to the army, and have neither been contemplated nor authorized by any orders whatsoever; the perpetrators of them, whether officers or soldiers, will be visited with a punishment which they will have reason to remember; and any officer or soldier absent from the limits of his camp found in any house whatever, without a written pass from his division or brigade commander, will be considered a pillager and treated accordingly. Army corps commanders will immediately establish mounted patrols, under charge of commissioned officers, which shall scour the whole country for 5 miles around their camps at least once every day, and at different hours, to bring into their respective commands all persons absent without proper authority, or who are engaged in any interruption of citizens living in the country; and commanding officers of regiments, or smaller separate commands, will be held responsible that neither officers nor men shall be absent from camp without proper authority.

By command of Major-General Pope:
R. O. SELFRIDGE,
Assistant Adjutant-General.

(O. R., 12, part 3, 573)

Admittedly, Pope belatedly takes more responsibility for his soldiers' behavior than Taylor did in Mexico, but through his General Orders Nos. 5, 7, and 11, Pope clearly created an organizational climate in which soldiers' violations of noncombatant rights should have been no surprise. In this regard, it was the same organizational climate Pope had served in under Taylor in Mexico.

DIFFERENT EXPERIENCES

Officers who served exclusively under Scott or under both Taylor and Scott in Mexico often had a more conciliatory attitude toward civilians and private

John Pope. Library of Congress, Prints and Photographs Division, reproduction number LC-B8172-2136 DLC (b&w film neg.).

property. George McClellan, who served primarily under Scott, held views so consistent with the limited approach that he even shared them with the enemy. On July 11, 1862, he wrote Hill Carter, the Virginian owner of a great estate near Malvern Hill, expressing his regret for the inconvenience and loss Carter had suffered because of the Federal army during McClellan's Peninsula Campaign. McClellan firmly stated, "I have not come here to wage war upon noncombatants, upon private property, nor upon the domestic institutions of the land" (K. Williams 250).

On July 7, McClellan expressed the same belief in a letter to President Lincoln, arguing that

> neither confiscation of property, political executions of persons, territorial organization of States, [n]or forcible abolition of slavery should be contemplated for a moment. In prosecuting the war all private property and unarmed persons should be strictly protected, subject only to the necessity of military operations. All private property taken for military use should be paid or receipted for; pillage

and waste should be treated as high crimes; all unnecessary tres-
pass sternly prohibited, and offensive demeanor towards citizens
promptly rebuked. (Boatner 380)

McClellan's letter reads like a blow-by-blow counter to Pope's orders advocat-
ing a harsher course (Catton, *Lincoln's Army* 152).

George Meade, who had served first under Taylor and then under Scott,
appears to have adopted Scott's view. When Meade was ordered to seize the
property of a Confederate sympathizer, he confessed shame for his cause, believing the North should prosecute the war "like the afflicted parent who is
compelled to chastise his erring child, and who performs the duty with a sad
heart" (Donald 44–45).

Pope's opponent at the time he issued these orders was Robert E. Lee,
a man who had served primarily under Scott in Mexico. Lee found Pope to
be a "miscreant" and wrote Stonewall Jackson: "I want Pope suppressed. The
course indicated in his orders if the newspapers report them correctly cannot
be permitted and will lead to retaliation on our part. You had better notify him
the first opportunity" (Dowdey and Manarin 239). Lee went on to protest the
actions of one of Pope's subordinates, Brigadier General Adolph von Steinwehr, who arrested five citizens of Luray, Virginia, and announced that whenever a guerrilla killed a soldier of his, one of the hostages would be shot unless
the locals delivered the guerrilla to the Federal commander. Douglas Southall Freeman concludes, "For no other adversary in the entire war did Lee have
anything that approached the contempt and personal dislike he had for Pope"
(*Lee* 2:264).

Of course, Pope and Taylor have their apologists, and it is true that Pope
tried to correct the situation with General Orders No. 19. Likewise, Ulysses
Grant argues that Taylor "was opposed to anything like plundering by the
troops" (39). Leaders, however, are responsible for more than just themselves.
They are responsible for the climate they set in their organizations, and they
set that climate by both actions and inactions (FM 22-100, 3-19). Taylor failed
to create the disciplined climate in northern Mexico that would have prevented
inappropriate treatment of civilians and private property. Pope, suffering perhaps from his experience under Taylor, made the same error in the Civil War.

George Meade and Missed Opportunity

Like Pope, George Meade served as one of Zachary Taylor's topographical engineers in Mexico and would be influenced by Taylor's generalship. Meade was with Taylor at Monterey, an American victory to be sure, but not a decisive one. The Mexican army under Pedro Ampudia would be spared to fight another day. Many criticized Taylor for not inflicting more damage on the Mexicans. Meade, however, sided with Taylor's decision. In the Civil War, Meade would win a great victory at Gettysburg, but his opponent, Robert E. Lee, would also escape to fight another day. Like Taylor, Meade would face severe criticism for not exploiting his victory. Perhaps he was just following the example he had seen in Mexico.

MONTEREY

Taylor arrived at Monterey on September 19, 1846, and attacked the following day. He divided his force, with William Worth conducting a flank attack from the west while Taylor attacked from the front. Both attacks succeeded, but only after three days of hard fighting and many casualties. On September 24, Ampudia offered to surrender Monterey under the condition that he be permitted to withdraw his force unmolested and that an eight-week armistice would go into effect. Surprisingly to many, Taylor agreed.

Taylor was concerned about his ability to keep fighting because he had lost some 800 men to battle casualties and sickness, had expended much ammunition, and was about 125 miles from his base. President James Polk did not share Taylor's concern and ordered the armistice nullified. Polk claimed Taylor had "violated express orders." Taylor had the enemy "in his power" and should have made prisoners of them all, taken away their weapons, put them on parole, and pressed on into the interior of Mexico. In Polk's mind, doing so "would probably have ended the war with Mexico" (J. Eisenhower, *So Far* 149).

Taylor's decision was the subject of considerable debate among his staff. Meade was one who strongly supported it. He cited the strength of the enemy and their defenses, the possibility of enemy reinforcements, and the disorganized and crippled status of Taylor's army. Meade wrote his wife, "For my part . . . I was exceedingly rejoiced; many of our brave fellows slept in a nameless grave, for the bodies of some were never recovered; and any one who for four days and nights is in constant state of exposure to fire-arms of all descriptions will be very well satisfied to terminate so disagreeable an occupation" (Cleaves, *Meade* 36).

In 1863, Meade would find himself in a similar circumstance at Gettysburg. This time he would not be a staff officer observing the decision but the commander who would have to make it. He would follow a logic and a course similar to those he had seen exercised by Taylor.

GETTYSBURG

Meade assumed command of the Army of the Potomac under very difficult circumstances. Robert E. Lee had just defeated Joe Hooker at Chancellorsville and had launched his second invasion into Northern territory. The Federal army had pursued Lee and was in Frederick, Maryland, but there appeared to be no strategic plan for what to do next. Amid this crisis, Meade was ordered on June 27, 1863, to take command of the Army of the Potomac. The order advised him, "Considering the circumstances, no one ever received a more important command." It was not a position Meade had sought, and he was overwhelmed and intimidated by the responsibility. In acknowledging the order, Meade replied, "As a soldier I obey it, and to the utmost of my ability will execute it." Meade described the order as "totally unexpected" and confessed "ignorance of the exact condition of the troops and position of the enemy" (Stackpole 82–84). In such circumstances, Meade would resolve to play it safe.

Like Monterey, Gettysburg was a three-day fight. The first day was an unplanned meeting engagement, which boiled down to a contest to see which side could bring up reinforcements the fastest. July 1 ended in a Confederate victory, but the Federals were able to remain in control of the key terrain of Cemetery Hill.

On July 2, Lee ordered James Longstreet to make the main attack against Meade's south flank. In the nick of time, Federal forces arrived at Little Round Top and held the position. The second day ended for the most part as a draw.

On the third day, Lee ordered a massive attack on the Federal center. The attack, including the famous Pickett's Charge, was repulsed, and the Federals could claim victory on the third day and for the overall battle.

Now the question became what to do with the victory. Both sides had been badly hurt, with Lee suffering 28,063 losses and Meade 23,049 (Boatner 339). The two armies lay facing each other "like spent lions nursing their wounds" (Randall 523–524). Meade was personally exhausted. After the battle, a newspaper reporter found him "stooping and weary," and Meade's biographer describes him as "a picture of sorry discomfort" (Cleaves, *Meade* 169). Meade was in no mood to exploit his victory, and Lee began withdrawing back into Virginia.

Lincoln, however, had other ideas. He announced Meade's success to the nation in restrained tones, withholding from Meade the thanks and praise he had lavished on Ulysses Grant after his victory at Vicksburg (Cleaves, *Meade* 171). Lincoln thought Meade's work was unfinished. It was not time to celebrate yet.

Like Taylor, Meade commanded an army that was battered by its victory. The men were tired from days of marching and fighting. Dead and wounded soldiers and damaged and discarded equipment filled the battlefield and had to be recovered. Many veteran soldiers, as well as key leaders such as John Reynolds and Winfield Scott Hancock, were killed or wounded (Cleaves, *Meade* 172–173).

One can only imagine Meade's psychological state. Bruce Catton paints a vivid picture:

Federal dead at Gettysburg. Library of Congress, Prints and Photographs Division, reproduction number LC-B8184-7964-A DLC (b&w film neg.).

Meade was on the road with his troops, an infinitely weary man with dust on his uniform and his gray beard, feeling responsibility as a paralyzing weight. He had been one of the few men who could have lost the war irretrievably in one day, and he had managed to avoid the mistakes that would have lost it. He would continue to avoid mistakes, even if he had to miss opportunity. . . . Meade could see all the things that might go wrong. (*Glory Road* 327–328)

Like Polk, Lincoln did not see these challenges, only the opportunity. Meade was instructed that "the opportunity to attack [Lee's] divided forces should not be lost. The President is urgent and anxious that your army should move against [Lee] by forced marches" (Cleaves, *Meade* 178).

In the end, however, Meade's halfhearted attempt to pursue Lee was of no consequence. Lee, like Ampudia, escaped to fight another day. Lincoln was beside himself. He wrote Meade, "I do not believe you appreciate the magnitude of the misfortune involved in Lee's escape. He was within your easy grasp, and to have closed upon him would, in connection with our other late successes, have ended the war. As it is, the war will be prolonged indefinitely" (Cleaves, *Meade* 185).

Like Taylor, Meade had his defenders. Chief among them were engineer Gouverneur Warren and artilleryman Henry Hunt. Still, many historians share Lincoln's view that, after Gettysburg, Meade lost an opportunity to end the war (Stackpole 306).

AUDACITY

Successful generals must be audacious. Neither Taylor nor Meade was. K. Jack Bauer concludes that "as badly mauled as [Taylor's] army had been, it was not in much worse shape than Ampudia's and had the psychological advantage which goes with the attacker. But Zachary Taylor was not an aggressive general though he was a very stubborn fighter. He clearly never fully recognized that the moment to attack was when your enemy was as tired as you were" (100). Edward Stackpole makes a similar observation about Meade, writing, "Some generals play it safe, forgetting perhaps that war is far from being a safe enterprise. Others take calculated risks when large results are possible. The great Captains have been those who audaciously and aggressively discounted the odds, whether actual or imagined, and by their boldness won important victories. . . . Meade was not [that kind of general]" (306–307). Maybe if he had a different example at Monterey, he would have been.

Jefferson Davis and the Bad Example

Brigadier General Jefferson Davis, U.S. Army, is an interesting footnote in the study of the Mexican War and the Civil War. The first point of note is obviously the name he shares with his more famous Confederate counterpart. The other unusual condition is that unlike most of the other Civil War generals who served in Mexico as young officers, Davis's Mexican War experience was as an enlisted man. From that perspective, he bore witness to his regimental commander strike his brigade commander. Uncannily, Davis would go on to murder his own commanding officer in the Civil War.

GENERAL LANE

Seeking adventure, young Davis enlisted in the Clark County Guards in Indiana at the age of eighteen. He learned quickly, showed good leadership qualities, and was soon promoted to corporal. On July 9, 1846, Davis embarked with his regiment for the voyage to Mexico. Upon arrival, they occupied Camp Belknap and commenced to drill. From Camp Belknap, the regiment eventually moved on to Reynosa, Camp Butler, and finally to Agua Nueva, where it prepared for its initial combat. But first there was trouble.

Colonel James Lane was the tough, ambitious, and aggressive commander of Davis's Third Indiana Regiment. He had a reputation for being a martinet. Lane's superior was General Joseph Lane, commander of the Indiana Brigade.

The two had a rocky past, and on February 20 they again were arguing. The tensions escalated quickly.

Colonel Lane had the regiment drawn up in a square, and within this formation he was discussing his desire to remove two officers from his regiment. General Lane stood just outside the square, listening. General Lane finally entered the square to "make a statement of his understanding of the matter," but Colonel Lane took issue with something the general had said. General Lane responded that "he did not care if the Colonel believed it or not" (Hughes and Whitney 11). More angry words were exchanged, and then General Lane took a swing at Colonel Lane. Colonel Lane "dodged the blow and struck the General in the face" (Hughes and Whitney 11). The two men were pulled apart, and General Lane stormed off, only to return shortly with a loaded musket.

General Lane demanded, "Are you ready, Colonel Lane?" to which the colonel responded by ordering a soldier to load his musket, and replied, "I soon can be." The soldier and several others loaded their muskets, and Colonel Lane reached for the weapon, but before matters could get worse, General Lane's guards intervened and led the general away. All the while, General Lane shouted challenges over his shoulder to Colonel Lane. It was a tense scene. One witness recalled, "I have no doubt the General would have killed the Colonel (General Lane was an excellent shot), and as little doubt fifty musket charges would have found lodgement in the General's body knowing as I do, the temper of the men of the Third Indiana at that time" (Hughes and Whitney 11).

Summarizing the incident, Davis's biographers Nathaniel Hughes and Gordon Whitney note:

> Certainly this experience impacted young Corporal Davis. He had witnessed his regimental commander strike his brigade commander. He watched General Lane leave the scene to arm himself and return prepared to kill Colonel Lane. How he perceived the incident, how he and his friend [Captain Tom] Gibson and others thought it should have been resolved can be seen, arguably, in Davis's confrontation with Gen. William Nelson fifteen years later. The similarity of the incidents cannot be dismissed. (11)

GENERAL NELSON

En route home from the war, Davis learned he had been appointed to West Point, but a procedural fiasco robbed him of his chance. To soften the blow, the War Department commissioned Davis directly as a second lieutenant. He remained in the service and rose rapidly during the Civil War, performing admirably at Pea Ridge and winning a promotion to brigadier general of the U.S. Volunteers in May 1862. Trouble, however, would soon cross Davis's path.

On August 12, Davis left his unit for twenty days of sick leave at his father-in-law's house in Indianapolis. While he was gone, Confederate forces under Edmund Kirby Smith invaded Kentucky. Defense of the key city of Louisville was the responsibility of Major General William Nelson.

Nelson had a reputation. He was a huge man, standing six feet four inches tall and weighing over 300 pounds. He had a temper to match his size and was nicknamed "Bull." One observer wrote, "Nelson was a martinet in matters of detail, brave and impulsive, but a man of strong passions, which he did not attempt to control. He was popular, some would say greatly beloved by the common soldier, but his conduct towards his subordinate officers was brusque, and often tyrannical and overbearing" (Hughes and Whitney 21).

Davis followed events from Indianapolis and realized his duty was with his division. He reported to Department of the Ohio commander Major General Horatio Wright, who ordered him to Louisville. He arrived on September 21. Nelson had arrived just earlier on September 18.

Nelson made quick use of the experienced Davis, assigning him the task of organizing the motley assortment of local volunteers. It was a thankless job, and Davis undoubtedly had hoped for something better. He also knew whatever he could do to organize the Home Guards was going to be a near-futile exercise, and he did little to pursue it. Word got to Nelson that Davis had been "sitting on heaters most of the time for the last four days," and he called Davis to his headquarters in the Galt House for a report (Hughes and Whitney 107–108).

According to James Fry, the encounter began with Nelson asking, "Well, Davis, how are you getting along with your command?"

Davis replied, "I don't know."

"How many regiments have you organized?" asked Nelson.

Again Davis said, "I don't know."

"How many companies have you?" pressed Nelson.

"I don't know," said Davis, in what Fry describes as a "seemingly care-less tone."

"But you should know," said Nelson, rising to his feet. "I am disappointed in you, General Davis. I selected you for this duty because you are an officer of the Regular Army, but I find I made a mistake."

The argument continued to escalate. Davis demanded "the courtesy due to my rank," to which Nelson replied, "You are relieved from duty here and you will proceed to Cincinnati and report to General Wright." Davis challenged Nelson's authority to impose such a measure and left the room "highly incensed by the treatment he had received."

Nonetheless, Davis left Louisville that night, joined company with General Stephen Burbridge, who had also been relieved by Nelson, and reported to Wright in Cincinnati. Wright temporarily assigned Davis to a command in front of Covington and Newport, Kentucky.

Ultimately, the Federal forces under Don Carlos Buell successfully secured Louisville, and thus Buell would be superseding Nelson in command. Wright undoubtedly figured it would now be safe to return Davis to Louisville. In the midst of all this, one witness alleges overhearing a group of Indiana officers and politicians plotting to provoke the volatile Nelson into a confrontation and use the ensuing melee as an excuse to shoot Nelson.

On the heels of this alleged meeting, Davis arrived at the Galt House. An observer reported that he "looked pale and was evidently laboring under unusual excitement." Davis intercepted Nelson in the lobby and demanded, "General Nelson, I want to know why you disgraced me by placing me in arrest."

The two exchanged words, and Nelson said, "Go away, you damned puppy. I don't want anything to do with you."

With that, Davis crumpled up a blank visiting card he had found lying on the hotel desk and flicked it into Nelson's face. With that, Nelson slapped Davis in the face. Davis drew back, clenched his fist, and demanded an apology, to which Nelson responded by slapping him again and calling him a coward.

Davis said, "I will see you again," and returned with a pistol. He found Nelson at the foot of the stairway and warned him, "Not another step further. General Nelson, take care of yourself." Nelson continued in Davis's direction.

Davis fired, the bullet striking Nelson just above the heart. Nelson staggered but continued up the stairs. He collapsed in the hallway at the top of the landing, saying, "I am murdered." In less than an hour Nelson was dead (Hughes and Whitney 98–115; Fried 14–16).

Remarkably, Davis was never brought to trial. A freakish combination of military emergency, a certain lack of sympathy for Nelson accompanied by the notion that Davis was acting in self-defense, and poor leadership by the proper authorities all spared Davis his seemingly due punishment. The murder has forever sullied Davis's historical reputation, but as for practical punishment, there was none.

TO BE EXPECTED?

Of course, one must be careful drawing too close a connection between Davis's Mexican and Civil War experiences, but the coincidence is certainly a strong one. As a witness to one incident and a participant in a related one, Davis clearly appears to be the victim of learning from a bad example. Accordingly, his otherwise impressive Civil War record has been tarnished.

Joe Hooker and the Administrative Side

Joe Hooker is most commonly remembered by the sobriquet "Fighting Joe Hooker." A series of Associated Press releases during the Seven Days battles were headed "Fighting-Joe Hooker," and newspapers all over the country simply removed the dash and used "Fighting Joe Hooker" as a subhead. The nickname stuck (Boatner 409). Hooker was an aggressive leader, but perhaps he should be better remembered for his contributions to the Army of the Potomac as "Administrative Joe Hooker" (Hebert 184). Indeed, Hooker's administrative accomplishments in the Civil War can be traced to his Mexican War experience.

CHIEF OF STAFF

Hooker certainly saw his share of combat in Mexico. He was brevetted three times for gallantry in action, but probably his most formative experience was to serve on the staffs of six different generals. Hooker would have an excellent opportunity in Mexico to learn the administrative and organizational aspects of the army.

Lieutenant Hooker's first assignment in Mexico was as brigade commissary officer for Brigadier General Persifor Smith, but this would be a brief posting. By the time Hooker reached Smith's headquarters, the army had been reinforced by numerous volunteers, often led by politically appointed generals of limited military experience. One of these was Brigadier General Thomas Hamer. To compensate for Hamer's shortcomings, Hooker was transferred to the general's headquarters to serve as his chief of staff (Hebert 26). Hooker fought with Hamer at Monterey and was brevetted to captain. Hamer died of illness in December 1846, but Hooker's performance caught the eye of Major General William Butler, who asked him to serve as his chief of staff.

While Hooker was serving under Butler, Winfield Scott launched his decisive campaign from Vera Cruz to Mexico City. In order to support such an effort, troops were withdrawn from various commands and transferred to Scott's army. Hooker was one of this number. On April 25, 1847, he was made chief of staff for Brigadier General George Cadwalladar. Hooker's biographer Walter Herbert speculates that "this transfer of duty was quite possibly made for the same reason that Hooker had previously been assigned to Hamer—to compensate for the General's lack of experience" (28).

Hooker fought under Butler at the National Bridge over the Antigua River and was brevetted to major. He was also once again transferred, this time to serve as assistant adjutant general to Major General Gideon Pillow. Hebert observes, "Pillow's lack of experience and ability in military affairs made Hooker a vital force in the division. Many people thought he furnished the brains, energy and industry at Pillow's headquarters" (29). Under Pillow, Hooker stormed the walls of Chapultepec, earning a brevet to lieutenant colonel.

After the capture of Mexico City, Hooker again was transferred, this time to the staff of Brigadier General Caleb Cushing. Hebert summarizes, "Once again Hooker was of great value in covering up for one of [President James] Polk's political appointments" (34).

Hooker's Mexican War experience gave him a full appreciation for staff operations, and his service under several commanders of dubious abilities gave him an opportunity to exercise great influence and responsibility beyond his rank. Surely Hooker had acquired a knowledge of the problems associated with handling 2,500 to 3,000 soldiers under battle conditions (Hebert 33). It was experience that would serve him well when he assumed command of the Army of the Potomac in January 1863.

ADMINISTRATIVE REFORMS

Hooker inherited the Army of the Potomac from Major General Ambrose Burnside, who had been soundly defeated at Fredericksburg the previous month. There were obvious deficiencies, and Hooker's first order of business was to set them straight (Hebert 172; S. Sears, *Chancellorsville* 63). His experience as a staff officer in Mexico would help him.

As Hooker began this process, one of his most important decisions was to appoint Major General Daniel Butterfield as his chief of staff. Having been a chief of staff himself, Hooker knew what the job required and what he wanted. In Butterfield, he found a skilled administrator who would help him with his reforms (S. Sears, *Chancellorsville* 63).

Hooker's administrative initiatives were far-reaching. He changed the army's organization by abolishing the four unwieldy grand divisions of two army corps each and creating a more streamlined structure of seven infantry and one cavalry corps. This consolidation of the army's cavalry under one commander was a significant step toward improving what had previously been a scattered and dysfunctional asset. Hooker addressed the problem of desertions by a carrot-and-stick approach that both tightened travel restrictions and offered amnesty to any soldier who returned to the army by April 1. In January, deserters had accounted for 30 percent of the army's absentees. By March 31 they were less than 4 percent. Hooker made several changes to improve morale. He instituted an enlightened furlough policy, instilled unit pride by implementing a system of distinctive unit badges first used by Phil Kearny in his division, and improved rations. Hooker announced, "My men shall be fed before I am fed, and before any of my officers are fed" (S. Sears, *Chancellorsville* 73). Hooker's reforms even touched the press, insisting on stricter accountability and thereby reducing security leaks, by insisting on bylines. To oversee all these reforms, Hooker increased the powers of his inspector-generals (S. Sears, *Chancellorsville* 62–75).

But Stephen Sears considers one of Hooker's developments "as important as any he made during his reorganizing efforts." This was to appoint Colonel George Sharpe as the head of his Bureau of Military Information. Sharpe was to be Hooker's chief of intelligence. It fell to Sharpe "to develop virtually from scratch a coherent, reliable, intelligence-gathering operation" (S. Sears, *Chancellorsville* 69).

The problem was that prior to Sharpe, there was no system to collect and analyze all-source intelligence. Allan Pinkerton, George McClellan's intelligence chief, had simply collected raw information and passed it on to the commander in bulky reports, with no effort to evaluate or analyze it. Moreover,

Colonel George Sharpe and other members of the Bureau of Military Information. Library of Congress, Prints and Photographs Division, reproduction number LC-B8171-0213 DLC (b&w film neg.).

Pinkerton's intelligence system was almost exclusively reliant on a vast network of spies. In this regard, he gained impressive access to the Confederacy, with one of his men even winning the confidence of Confederate secretary of war Judah Benjamin (Catton, *Lincoln's Army* 121). Unfortunately, this single-source-type intelligence lacked the coordination and corroboration that are essential in gaining an accurate intelligence picture. As a result, Catton concludes that Pinkerton "ran perhaps the most unaccountably inefficient intelligence service an American army ever had" (*Hallowed Ground* 138).

Sharpe turned things around. For the first time, he coordinated the information from prisoners, deserters, contrabands, refugees, balloon observations, infantry and cavalry reports, and signal stations into an ordered and evaluated form. As a result, Stephen Sears concludes, "For the first time in its history, the Army of the Potomac had promise of a true picture of the Rebel army it was going to fight" (*Chancellorsville* 70).

THE RESULT

The final assessment of Hooker's administrative reforms was "a contribution to the Army of the Potomac more important than any of the fighting he had engaged in as division and corps commander." Indeed, Francis Walker, assistant adjutant general of the Second Corps, thought that during the period of Hooker's reforms, "[t]he Army of the Potomac never spent three months to better advantage" (Hebert 184). It was a result made possible in part by Hooker's grooming as a staff officer in Mexico.

WILLIAM SHERMAN
AND ROOM TO GROW

In June 1861, William Sherman and several other officers reported in person to President Abraham Lincoln. All had been told to ask for whatever positions they wanted. Sherman asked for and received the relatively low position of colonel of one of the ten new regiments of regulars that Congress had authorized.

On his way out of the White House, Sherman met his old West Point friend Irvin McDowell. McDowell, wearing his new uniform of a brigadier general, said, "Hello, Sherman. What did you ask for?"

"A colonelcy," replied Sherman.

"What?" exclaimed McDowell. "You should have asked for a brigadier general's rank. You're just as fit for it as I am."

"I know it," answered Sherman (Lewis 162).

Sherman was a major general by the time the war ended and made full general in 1869. His Atlanta Campaign and March to the Sea rank him second only to Grant as the military architect of the Federal victory.

For his part, McDowell was soundly defeated at First Manassas, was relieved of command as a result of poor performance at Second Manassas, and served out the rest of the war on boards and commissions in Washington and as commander of the unimportant Department of the Pacific. Obviously, there was more to Sherman's tart response to McDowell back in June 1861 than mere bravado.

CALIFORNIA

Sherman's service during the Mexican War was spent in California, far away from the real fighting. He served there with fellow future Federal generals E. O. C. Ord and Henry Halleck. By the time Sherman arrived in California, whatever fighting was to be done had already been handled by the navy. "No fighting," lamented Sherman. "That's too bad after coming so far" (Marszalek 62).

Sherman spent much of his time in California traveling and exploring, often with Ord. He knew he was missing the action. "To hear of the war in Mexico and the brilliant deeds of the army . . . and I out in California" (Marszalek 67). Sherman felt "perfectly banished" (Marszalek 68).

SLOW START

When the Civil War broke out, there were rumors that Sherman, like many of his fellow West Pointers, would receive a high initial position. In response, Sherman wrote his brother, John, on May 24, 1861, "Really I do not conceive myself qualified for Quarter Master General, or Major General. To attain either station I would prefer a previous schooling with large masses of troops in the field, one which I lost in the Mexican War by going to California" (Simpson and Berlin 92). In a meeting with President Lincoln, Sherman expressed his "extreme desire to serve in a subordinate capacity, and in no event to be left in a superior command" (Flood 58). While Sherman's self-assessment is refreshing, it is also important to note how the definition of "large masses of troops" would evolve. By Civil War standards, Scott's entire Mexican War army would have barely made a respectable corps (Doughty 92).

Sherman could not help noticing that others whom he believed were unqualified were not imitating his discipline. "The appointment of Pope, Reeder, Banks, Frémont, etc will afford Bragg & Davis & Beauregard the liveliest pleasure. The North has so decided an advantage in men for the Ranks, that it is a pity to balance the chances, by choice of leaders" (Simpson and Berlin 97). Sherman knew what was at stake. Concerning the appointment of leaders, he wrote his brother, "The magnitude of interests at issue now, will admit of no experiments" (Simpson and Berlin 93).

Sherman held himself to this same high standard. He knew his limited experience in California had not prepared him as well as active fighting in Mexico would have, and he was unwilling to "experiment" with the lives of soldiers. Sherman would pay his dues, starting off modestly, gaining experience, and rising when he was ready.

THE EXCEPTION

While Sherman grew into positions of greater responsibility, others courted them before they were ready or were thrust into them. Herman Hattaway and Archer Jones note that on the eve of the war, "The U.S. Army rolls included virtually no general officers fit for field duty. The swelling size of both armies forced Lincoln and Davis to elevate numerous individuals to that lofty martial status" (29).

Lincoln appointed some generals, such as John McClernand, for political reasons. Others, such as McDowell, possessed what Hattaway and Jones call "surface qualifications" (31). Still others, such as Robert Patterson, were superannuated. Some had militia connections, such as Benjamin Butler. The Confederacy had officers who were appointed or advanced based on similar considerations, such as Gideon Pillow and John Pemberton.

As casualties took their toll, junior officers were often promoted before they were ready, many reaching their highest level of incompetence in accordance with the Peter Principle. Dick Ewell is a good example, showing "an inability to make the transition from a closely controlled division commander under Stonewall Jackson to a corps commander under Lee's discretionary orders" (Boatner 269).

Sherman avoided these troubles because he realistically assessed himself. He knew that his experience in California had not prepared him like experience in Mexico would have. He was willing to start the war at a moderate rank and make up the difference. He was wise to do so. T. Harry Williams cites

Sherman as one of the two "most outstanding examples of growth and origi-nality among the Northern generals" (Donald 50). (Grant is the other.)

Some generals excelled in the Civil War because of what they learned in Mexico. Sherman excelled because he was smart enough to recognize what he had not learned.

Henry Halleck and the Military Executive

Like Sherman's, Henry Halleck's Mexican War experience would be in California. There Halleck held such political-military and administrative positions as secretary of state, chief of staff, and lieutenant governor in the Mexican city of Mazatlan (Hattaway and Jones 54). His service in California was exemplary, demonstrating "great energy, high administrative qualities, excellent judgment and admirable adaptability to his varied and onerous duties." Bennett Riley, the military governor, was moved to declare, "Whatever success my administration has attained is mainly owing to the efficient aid rendered by Captain Henry W. Halleck, the secretary of state. To him should be the applause. He has never failed me" (Eldredge). In such a capacity, Halleck saw almost no combat, but Herman Hattaway and Archer Jones conclude that in the Civil War, "Halleck's executive experience in California proved quite useful" (63).

COMMAND OF THE MISSOURI DEPARTMENT

On November 19, 1861, Halleck replaced John C. Frémont as commander of the Missouri Department. Frémont had made a mess of things. Hattaway and Jones consider Frémont "a disastrous failure as a military executive," whose "temperament was ill adapted for management" and who had produced "a complex and ineffective administration in Missouri" (55). Halleck considered it "complete chaos." He found troops unpaid and without proper uniforms and weapons and the Confederates "in possession of nearly one-half of the State" (Hattaway and Jones 64).

In terms of finance, supply, and organization, the department was in a shambles. Under Halleck, however, "fraudulent contracts were annulled; useless stipendaries were dismissed; a colossal staff hierarchy, with more titles than brains was disbanded; . . . the construction of fantastic fortifications was suspended; and in a few weeks order reigned in Missouri" (Hattaway and Jones 55).

Halleck reported that the "machinery for the supply of the Army is rapidly getting into working order" and that he was "in hourly communication with headquarters of divisions" thanks to the telegraph. Even Confederate President Jefferson Davis noted the difference, observing that "the Federal forces are not hereafter, as heretofore, to be commanded by Pathfinders [Frémont's nickname] and holiday soldiers but by men of military education and experience in war" (Hattaway and Jones 64). For Halleck, that "experience in war" had been in an administrative capacity in California, but it was exactly what the current situation in Missouri required.

Now Halleck could turn his attention to implement General in Chief George McClellan's order to consolidate the Federal hold on Missouri and concentrate "the mass of the troops on or near the Mississippi" in preparation for future operations (Hattaway and Jones 55). In this regard, Halleck had also benefited from the Mexican War by gaining an appreciation for strategic lines of operation. Winfield Scott, Halleck wrote, had been "truly strategic" in his movement to Vera Cruz, and Halleck greatly admired Scott's turning movement at Cerro Gordo, which cut off Santa Anna's line of retreat. On the contrary, Halleck disapproved of Zachary Taylor's line of operation, noting that "Santa Anna, from his central position fought, with the same troops, the battles of Buena Vista and Cerro Gordo" (Hattaway and Jones 16).

Halleck made use of this understanding of lines of operation one night in late December or early January when he was strategizing with George Cullum, his chief of staff, and William Sherman, his fellow veteran of California. Sherman recalled that

> General Halleck had a map on his table with a large pencil in his hand, and asked, "Where is the rebel line?" Cullum drew the pencil through Bowling Green, forts Donelson and Henry, and Columbus, Kentucky. "That is their line," said Halleck. "Now where is

the proper place to break it?" And either Cullum or I said, "*Natu-rally* the centre." Halleck drew a line perpendicular to the other near its middle, and it coincided with the general course of the Tennessee River; and he said, "That's the true line of operations" (Sherman 1:248)

Halleck had correctly ascertained the Confederate weakness on the Tennessee and Cumberland rivers and developed a plan to "turn Columbus and force the abandonment of Bowling Green" (Hattaway and Jones 65). "This line of the Cumberland or Tennessee is the great central line of the Western theatre of war," Halleck wrote McClellan (Nevins 6:17). The result of this strategy was the decisive Federal victories at Forts Henry and Donelson.

GENERAL IN CHIEF

Indeed, Halleck excelled "in making war on the map" (Hattaway and Jones 77), but he was "an incompetent leader of field armies" (Boatner 367), as his actions at Corinth, Mississippi, would demonstrate. There it took him almost a month to advance just twenty miles, stopping to entrench at the end of each day's march and ultimately planning to besiege the city. Before Halleck finally was ready to begin his bombardment, the Confederates withdrew. Rather than push on into Mississippi after them, Halleck elected to consolidate his gains (Boatner 176). Then he broke up his massive army by sending detachments to various other commanders, thus allowing the Confederates to camp unmolested at Tupelo (Ballard, *Mississippi* 13). Clearly, Halleck's talents lay as a military manager rather than as a practitioner, and he was ultimately called to Washington to serve as general in chief.

As general in chief, Halleck continued his managerial functions but on a broader and higher plane. His experience as secretary of state and military governor during the Mexican War had prepared him for the political aspects of his new job. Indeed, Bruce Catton notes that Halleck's political background allowed him to "understand that the [Lincoln] administration's chief problems were political rather than military" (*Hallowed Ground* 270). President Lincoln could use Halleck to perpetuate Lincoln's desire to present a facade of impo-

Henry Halleck. Library of Congress, Prints and Photographs Division, reproduction number LC-B8172-6377 DLC (b&w film neg.).

tence, implying to critics that he exercised little power and entrusted much to military professionals. Whenever Lincoln fired a general, it was Halleck who would sign the order and thus took the blame. If critics questioned Lincoln, the president would say, "I wish not to control. That I leave to General Halleck" (Hattaway and Jones 287–288). The political acumen Halleck had learned in California served him well in the Civil War.

When Ulysses Grant assumed command as general in chief in March 1864, Halleck's role was reduced to chief of staff, another position he had held in California. Again, however, his administrative service was valuable, allowing Grant to take to the field while Halleck remained in Washington. There Halleck was part of "a rear-area team that grasped the delicate balance between theater objectives and the logistical support required to achieve them" (Conn 264). Halleck acted as a link between Grant and the War Department bureaus. Accordingly, Grant did not have to fight for support from obstinate bureau chiefs. He just told Halleck what he needed, and Halleck ensured compliance (Donovan et al. 303). Halleck also helped Grant control the seventeen different commands and 533,000 men who fell underneath him. Halleck freed Grant from writing detailed instructions to each subordinate. Instead, the dispatches of departmental generals were sent to Halleck, who often summarized their contents before forwarding them to Grant. In turn, Grant would often send Halleck general concepts, which Halleck would then turn into detailed instructions for the subordinates. Without Halleck's astute performance of these administrative functions, "Grant could not have devoted any attention to strategic planning" (T. Williams, *Lincoln* 302).

Halleck was also very valuable to Lincoln. T. Harry Williams considers Halleck to have "had the happy faculty of being able to communicate civilian ideas to a soldier and military ideas to a civilian and make both them understand what he was talking about. He could interpret Lincoln's strategic concepts to Grant and Grant's military language to the President. Because of Halleck, Lincoln and Grant never misunderstood each other, as Lincoln and McClellan had" (*Lincoln* 301). Obviously, Halleck could draw on his experience in California to help with this civil-military communication.

Like Sherman, Halleck had not gained combat experience during the Mexican War, but he did benefit from his time in California, and the experience did have a marked impact on his Civil War career. In California, Halleck had learned administrative and managerial skills that would allow him to play "a major role in the administration of the Civil War" (Boatner 367). Also, he had indirectly learned to appreciate strategy by his study of Scott and Taylor, especially with regard to lines of operation, and as head of the Missouri Department, he would apply what he had learned. However, Halleck's lack of actual operational experience would ill-prepare him for the role of field commander in the Civil War, and he was ineffective in such a capacity.

Both Sherman and Halleck had similar noncombat experiences in California. Sherman recognized this limitation, and by starting off slowly, he grew into an outstanding field commander in the Civil War. Conversely, Halleck stuck with what he had learned in California and made his mark in the Civil War as an administrator.

Henry Hunt and the
Organization of Artillery

Napoleon had taught that "it is with artillery that war is made," and a series of forward-looking secretaries of war had agreed and ensured that at the time of the Mexican War, the U.S. Army had the finest artillery in the world (J. Eisenhower, *So Far* 379–380). Indeed, artillery was such a key factor in Mexico that it single-handedly accounted for victories such as Palo Alto (Bauer 57). Lieutenant Henry Hunt contributed to this pivotal role of artillery in Mexico, and he would apply what he learned there later as chief of artillery for the Army of the Potomac.

WITH DUNCAN IN MEXICO

In 1839, Secretary of War Joel Poinsett ordered the establishment of a camp of artillery instruction at Trenton, New Jersey. One company of each artillery regiment was to be sent there and equipped as a battery of light artillery. For the Second U.S. Artillery, this was A Company, commanded by Lieutenant James Duncan (Simpson 316). In August 1845, Duncan, now a captain, deployed his battery from New York Harbor to join Zachary Taylor in Mexico. Quickly, Duncan would establish an excellent reputation based on his actions at Palo Alto, Resaca de la Palma, and Molino del Rey.

One of Duncan's lieutenants was Henry Hunt, who would especially distinguish himself at Chapultepec. There infantry was burrowing its way with picks and crowbars through the city's walls in a house-to-house advance, while mountain howitzers fired from rooftops on either side of the road. Still, Mexican artillery was able to sweep the road from behind a barricade with a firing port. Into the fire-swept street, Hunt and eight men advanced with one gun. In what Brigadier General William Worth would call a "brilliant exhibition of courage and conduct," Hunt pushed his gun up to the enemy's position and, firing "muzzle to muzzle," reduced the resistance (Henry, *Mexican War* 365).

Duncan emerged from Mexico as "the premier American artillerist" (Lawrence). Hunt was both friend and pupil of Duncan and would ultimately take command of Duncan's battery. This experience of learning at the hand of such a master artillerist would prepare Hunt well for assuming his Civil War responsibilities.

WITH THE ARMY OF THE POTOMAC

Bruce Catton describes Hunt as a "keen student of the new science of gunnery" (*Glory Road* 36), and Hunt clearly took full advantage of the opportunity to learn under Duncan. Hunt would put the lessons he had learned into application as chief of artillery for the Army of the Potomac. It was a role to which he was well suited because of his skill as an organizer. Indeed, when Hunt inherited the Army of the Potomac's artillery, it was not organized as he wanted it to be. Hunt had an unwavering belief in massed fires (Catton, *Glory Road* 36; Henry, *Mexican War* 365). One of his most important organizational initiatives would be to configure the Army of the Potomac's artillery to make such fires possible.

Duncan's tutelage had well prepared Hunt for his Civil War responsibilities, and it was a good thing for him that it did. Hunt assessed that by the time of the Civil War, "[t]he field artillery was in an unsatisfactory condition. The high reputation it had gained in Mexico was followed by the active and persistent hostility of the War Department, which almost immediately dismounted three-fourths of its authorized batteries" (259).

This interwar neglect was exacerbated by the initial misuse of artillery in the Army of the Potomac under General George McClellan's period of command. Under McClellan, artillery batteries were assigned to divisions, with each division then relinquishing two batteries to form a corps reserve. Control of the guns was inconsistent. Arrangements varied from divisions retaining control, to divisions giving control to the corps, to a combination of the two. In battle, this lack of unity of command meant confused and countermanded orders. As a result, artillery was ineffective.

In September 1862, Hunt became the chief of artillery for the Army of the Potomac, and within a year he was able to effect a reorganization of the artillery and centralize its command. Hunt grouped batteries into brigades and placed them under the leadership of a corps chief of artillery. Additionally, the Artillery Reserve, a body of 100 guns, including the horse and siege cannon, was reorganized into five artillery brigades. The reserve could be dispatched partially or collectively to reinforce batteries (*Echoes* 297). Hunt had brought about his vision of massed artillery.

FREDERICKSBURG

But there was one lesson that Hunt seemed to forget as he stood with Major General Ambrose Burnside outside Fredericksburg, Virginia, in December 1862. Mass is not just mere numbers. It is concentrating effects at the decisive place and time (FM 3-0, 4-13). At Chapultepec, Hunt had just one gun, but he used it to great effect. At Fredericksburg, Hunt would have 140 guns but would not be able to achieve his desired effect. Mass is about effects, not numbers.

Burnside dispatched several parties of engineers to build bridges across the Rappahannock River at Fredericksburg. Burnside's chief engineer, Lieutenant Cyrus Comstock, instructed his men, "If enemy's fire is kept down, bridges to be thrown as soon as boats are unloaded; if too hot, wait till artillery silences it" (Goolrick 50–51). Defending Fredericksburg were Brigadier General William Barksdale and 1,600 men. Barksdale's Mississippians would indeed make it "too hot" for Comstock, so Burnside called on Hunt to exercise the second half of Comstock's contingency (Goolrick 50–51).

Hunt had over 140 artillery pieces, including Rodman three-inch rifles, ten- and twenty-pounder Parrotts, and a few four-and-a-half-inch siege guns. Of these, more than 100 would be ordered to fire fifty rounds each at the waterfront opposite the engineers (Catton, *Glory Road* 37).

The result was spectacular. Confederate artilleryman E. Porter Alexander observed from his vantage point on Marye's Heights:

> The city, except its steeples, was still veiled in the mist, which had settled in the valleys. Above it and in it incessantly showed the round white clouds bursting shells, and out of its midst there soon rose three or four columns of dense black smoke from houses set on fire by the explosions. The atmosphere was so perfectly calm and still that smoke rose vertically in great pillars for several hundred feet before spreading outward in black sheets. (Goolrick 52)

Likewise, Douglas Southall Freeman writes, "A furious bombardment it was. It swept the streets, it shattered houses, it shook the very hills" (*Lee's Lieutenants* 2:336)

But for all its fury—estimates range from 5,000 to 9,000 rounds fired—the bombardment did not drive out Barksdale's men. Finding shelter in the cellars of brick homes, the Confederates emerged virtually unharmed. When the engineers renewed their efforts, Barksdale's sharpshooters once again began delivering accurate fire from basement windows and piles of rubble. The Federal effort ceased once more.

Eventually, Hunt admitted that artillery alone could not dislodge the Confederates, and he suggested to Burnside that infantrymen be rowed across the river to clear the opposite shore. Burnside took the advice and established a makeshift amphibious assault. In the wake of this attack, Barksdale eventually conducted an orderly street-by-street withdrawal and rejoined the Confederate main body on Marye's Heights, but not until he had delayed Burnside for more than twelve hours and allowed the Confederates to prepare strong defenses and position reserves (Goolrick 53).

WHAT HAPPENED?

Fredericksburg indicated three key differences from the artillery experience that Hunt had in Mexico. First, unlike at Palo Alto, it would be nearly impossible in the Civil War for artillery to carry the day by itself. The infantry

Typical Parrott gun used in the Civil War. Library of Congress, Prints and Photographs Division, reproduction number LC-B8171-3283 DLC (b&w film copy neg.).

and the artillery would have to work in concert. Second, mass would not be merely a result of numbers. Hunt's success with a single gun at Chapultepec was a function of employment at the decisive time and place rather than overwhelming numbers. Finally, the successful use of artillery in an urban environment in Mexico was a result of very close in and deliberate targeting (Dougherty 16–17). At Fredericksburg, Catton notes that Hunt was taught "the lesson which artillerists have to learn anew in each generation—that a bombardment which will destroy buildings will not necessarily keep brave defenders from fighting on amid the wreckage" (*Glory Road* 38). The challenge of replicating the artillery's preeminent role in the Mexican War would continue to vex Hunt and his fellow artillerists in the Civil War. Stonewall Jackson would suffer the same frustration.

George Thomas
and the Rock

George Thomas's biographer Richard O'Connor makes a brief survey of the impact of the Mexican War on several Civil War generals and then boldly asserts, "But it is doubtful, on the face of their records, whether any learned their lessons in battle more thoroughly than George H. Thomas" (79). While O'Connor's conclusion may be somewhat overly enthusiastic, Thomas did have three very important experiences in Mexico that can account for certain aspects of his Civil War generalship. The first is the need for secure lines of supply. Thomas's close brush with logistic disaster under Zachary Taylor stands in sharp contrast with Ulysses Grant's positive experience under Winfield Scott. These different experiences partially explain Thomas's and Grant's diverging opinions about the pace of Thomas's operations at Nashville. Second, Thomas developed a dogged persistence. In Mexico, he would earn the nickname "Old Reliable" for his determination at Monterey (Cleaves, *Thomas* 34). In the Civil War, he would show the same steadiness as the "Rock of Chickamauga." Finally, Thomas learned that a key to this ability to stand fast is well-placed artillery. It was a lesson Thomas would learn at Buena Vista in Mexico and remember at Murfreesboro and Chickamauga in the Civil War.

LOGISTICAL SECURITY

While Grant learned from Scott that an army could cut loose from its communications and live off the land, other young officers who served in Mexico under Zachary Taylor learned something different. Taylor had ended up with his lines overextended at Fort Brown. While he managed to hold out, a more efficient and determined enemy could have intercepted Taylor's relief force and destroyed the isolated garrison at its leisure. Junior officers such as Thomas who witnessed this experience learned a lesson completely different than the audacity learned by Grant. Instead, Thomas developed an "innate store of caution and [the experience] helped to make him less an improviser than a leader who operated on fixed principles, with absolute readiness his first rule" (Cleaves, *Thomas* 28). In the Civil War, whenever Thomas was in independent command, he insisted on establishing fixed bases of supplies and making his lines of communication secure before advancing very deep into enemy territory.

The most notable example of this trait is Nashville. Grant repeatedly pressed Thomas to follow up his victory at Franklin with a headlong pursuit of John Hood's Confederates. Grant "threatened, harassed and nagged [Thomas] under conditions an officer of proven competence has seldom endured" (O'Connor 304), yet Thomas remained firmly convinced he must husband his force before acting. Thomas explained to Grant, "We can get neither reinforcements nor equipment at this great distance from the North very easily" (O'Connor 308–309). Obviously, Thomas was concerned about the same close call he witnessed Taylor suffer from extended lines of communication in Mexico.

"OLD RELIABLE" BECOMES THE "ROCK"

After Murfreesboro, Major General William Rosecrans marched southwest to try to capture the vital rail junction of Chattanooga. To counter, Confederate General Braxton Bragg deployed most of his troops at crossings of the Tennessee River northeast of Chattanooga, where he expected Rosecrans to attack. Instead, Rosecrans moved in three widely separated columns and was able to get to Bragg's rear and threaten his railroad supply line.

On September 9, 1863, Bragg abandoned Chattanooga and retreated southward. As his army passed through LaFayette, Georgia, he learned of the widely scattered condition of Rosecrans's army and planned an offensive to defeat the Federal forces in detail. At the same time, Rosecrans began ordering a concentration of his troops, realizing that his three isolated corps placed his army in danger.

By September 17, two of Rosecrans's corps were reunited and were moving north toward Lee and Gordon's Mill on Chickamauga Creek to join the third corps. Believing that the Federal troops at Lee and Gordon's Mill constituted the northernmost elements of Rosecrans's force, Bragg developed a battle plan to cross Chickamauga Creek north of the mill and drive the Federal troops back against the mountains to the southwest and away from Chattanooga.

On September 18, the Confederates attempted to seize crossing points on Chickamauga Creek. The Federals fought a delaying action that prevented the Confederates from reaching the left flank of the main Federal force, but Bragg did get across the Chickamauga by the end of the day.

These developments led Rosecrans to believe Bragg might try to get between the Federals and Chattanooga, so Rosecrans ordered Thomas to extend his corps lines northward to hold the left side of the line. On the morning of September 19, Thomas sent troops eastward from the Kelly farm to destroy what he thought was a small and isolated enemy force. Instead, the Federals encountered Confederate cavalrymen and ushered in a confused general engagement that lasted all day and spread southward for nearly four miles. Both Rosecrans and Bragg sent reinforcements to the fighting. At one point, the Confederates achieved a breakthrough and threatened to seize the LaFayette Road, but Federal reinforcements regained the lost ground. At the end of the day, the Federal troops had withstood repeated attacks without losing their connection to Chattanooga. That night they pulled back to a defensive position along the LaFayette Road, which they strengthened by constructing log breastworks. This sharp action was just the beginning for Thomas.

During the night of September 19 and early morning of September 20, Bragg divided his army into two wings, the right wing under Lieutenant General Leonidas Polk and the left wing under Lieutenant General James Longstreet. After a slow start, the Confederate attack picked up momentum, and by noon the Confederates had enveloped the center and right wings of the Federal army, sending Rosecrans, several of his principal subordinates, and many of their men into a retreat northward to Chattanooga.

In the midst of the chaos, Thomas was ordered to retreat (Hill, "Chickamauga" 655). He had received the same order in Buena Vista: "Retreat or you

George Thomas. Library of Congress, Prints and Photographs Division, reproduction number LC-B8172-6480 DLC (b&w film neg.).

are lost!" There "Thomas fulfilled the letter of the order by withdrawing his guns by the recoil of their discharge—reloading, firing and letting them spring back." All around him, regiments "crumpled and fled for the rear" (O'Connor 78). It was the same situation now, yet again Thomas held firm. According to Richard O'Connor, at that moment "disaster broke about [Thomas] like surf crashing into a wrecked ship, but his determination to hold the road to Chattanooga never wavered in the darkest moments of that afternoon" (44).

At first, Thomas did not realize the Federal right had vanished in the wake of the Confederate onslaught. He merely continued to defend on the left. By about midafternoon though, he knew that his corps had become the focal point of Bragg's entire army. He tenaciously held his ground, refusing to allow the Confederates to turn his right flank, plugging gaps as necessary, and judiciously repositioning forces as new threats appeared (Donovan et al. 278).

Critical to Thomas's defense was his artillery, which he had astutely emplaced along Horseshoe Ridge. O'Connor relates that "Thomas, the artillerist always, had placed his guns so they could rake the flank of any Confederate force assaulting the ridge," and that is exactly what happened (45). As in Mexico, Thomas had personally supervised the emplacement of the guns (Tucker, *Chickamauga* 25). O'Connor concludes: "Thomas, the young artillerist, learned lessons [at] ... Buena Vista he was never to forget, and they were to insure Federal victories on more than one battlefield. Even when commanding a corps or an army, Thomas would place the artillery himself and often direct its fire, if the moment were critical" (79).

Thomas's leadership was inspirational. For six hours he and his 25,000 men withstood the assaults of twice their number. Throughout it all, Thomas "only became calmer and more majestic," riding along his entire perimeter to lead by example and share the danger with his men (O'Connor 47). "He issued orders to restore the line in the quiet conversational tone that politeness prescribes for a ladies' drawing-room. It was the discipline of a lifetime concentrated on a moment" (Donovan et al. 278). At least part of that lifetime had been spent in another stoic defense at Monterey.

Eventually, Major General Gordon Granger would move his Reserve Corps to the sound of the guns and relieve Thomas. Thomas withdrew back toward Chickamauga to the safety of a gap in Missionary Ridge. As a result of Chickamauga, Thomas would replace Rosecrans as commander of the Army of the Cumberland. Before that, however, "Old Reliable" had a new nickname. From that point forward, Thomas would be the "Rock of Chickamauga." Timothy Donovan concludes that Thomas's stout defense demonstrated "grim determination in the face of great adversity" (Donovan et al. 279). Those who had been with Thomas in Mexico should not have been surprised. Coincidentally, among those who were with him at Buena Vista was Braxton Bragg, his captain then and his opponent now (Hill, "Chickamauga" 658).

PART TWO

THE CONFEDERATES

Robert E. Lee and Turning Movements Based on Reconnaissance

Emory Thomas writes of the Mexican War that "for the first time in American history, United States armies marched on foreign soil and fought battles in an alien land. Maps were few and often unreliable, and Mexican guides for obvious reasons were even fewer and even less reliable. What . . . commanders required of the Engineers was reconnaissance, accurate information about roads, rivers, terrain, and the enemy. Consequently Engineer officers very quickly made themselves indispensable and found themselves not only recommending routes and evaluating enemy positions but also offering informed advice about strategy and tactics" (*Lee* 115). British Major General Sir Frederick Maurice echoes that "at that time picked officers of the Engineers' Corps, itself a *corps d'elite*, performed many of the functions which today are assigned to the General Staff. They made reconnaissances, undertook the selection of positions, and prepared plans and orders for their general" (25).

One of these noble engineers was Captain Robert E. Lee. Lee's contributions to the American war effort in Mexico were phenomenal. General Winfield Scott would describe Lee as "the very best soldier I ever saw in the field," and suggested that in the event of war, the government should insure Lee's life for $5 million a year (Thomas, *Lee* 140). But if Lee's contribution to the war was great, the war contributed to Lee as well. Douglas Southall Freeman concluded the following with regard to the Mexican War's impact on Lee: "The relation of careful reconnaissance to sound strategy was impressed on Lee

by every one of the battles he saw in Mexico. . . . Lee had shown special aptitude for this work and he left Mexico convinced for all time that when battle
is imminent a thorough study of the ground is the first duty of the commanding officer. Reconnaissance became second nature to him" (*Lee* 1:296–297). It
was a lesson Lee carried with him into the Civil War.

CERRO GORDO

One of the most famous of Lee's Mexican War reconnaissance exploits was at
Cerro Gordo, the name of both a 1,000-foot-high hill and the town that lay
behind it. Seven miles to the east was another town named Plan del Rio. Both
are on north bank of the Rio del Plan, a river that runs east-west in a straight
line. The National Road joins the two towns but does not follow the banks
of the river. Instead, it meanders off to the northeast immediately after leaving Plan del Rio, and only later does it return and run along the river before
reaching Cerro Gordo.

Along that stretch where there was considerable space between the National Road and the river bluffs, Mexican commander Santa Anna had positioned three artillery batteries on prominent cliffs to command the National
Road approach. Santa Anna's main defensive position was on the hill of Cerro
Gordo, a couple of miles behind these artillery batteries. Americans approach-
ing Santa Anna along the National Road would be exposed to deadly fire.

The defense, however, had one weakness. To Santa Anna's left, or north,
flank was an extensive tract of wilderness, the vegetation being so thick that
Santa Anna had no reasonable observation in that direction. His flank was thus
vulnerable, but he was willing to accept this risk because he considered the
tangled woods impassable. Santa Anna's subordinates did not share this confidence, but in spite of their pleas to defend the flank, Santa Anna sent only
an observation post.

Scott wanted to avoid a costly frontal attack down the National Road.
Lieutenants Joe Johnston, P. G. T. Beauregard, and Zealous Tower had previously conducted reconnaissance of the area along the National Road and of the
Mexican artillery positions between the road and the river. What Scott needed
now was information about the potential route around Santa Anna's left flank.

Thus he dispatched a second reconnaissance mission led by Major John Smith, chief engineer, and Captain Robert E. Lee (J. Eisenhower, *Agent* 251–252).

Lee summarized the problem, writing that "the right of the Mexican line rested on the river at a perpendicular rock, unscalable by man or beast, and their left on impassable ravines; the main road was defended by field works containing thirty-five cannon; in their rear was the mountain of Cerro Gordo, surrounded by intrenchments in which were cannon and crowned by a tower overlooking all—it was around this army that it was intended to lead our troops" (Freeman, *Lee* 1:239). Slowly Lee worked his way up the ravines north of the river. The terrain was difficult, but Lee thought it would not be impossible to construct a crude road over it.

At one point Lee stopped at a spring to which a path led from the south. From the evidence of much traffic, Lee concluded he was at the rear of the Mexican left flank. Before long, he heard voices of Mexicans and saw a group of Mexican soldiers coming forward toward the spring. With just an instant to react, Lee dropped down behind a large brush-covered log close to the water. More and more Mexicans came and went, some sitting on the very log behind which Lee hid. Lee remained in this precarious position the remainder of the day. Not until darkness came did the last Mexican leave, and Lee was able to steal away (Freeman, *Lee* 1:239–241).

Upon returning to the American lines, Lee compared notes with Major Smith, who on his own reconnaissance had come to similar conclusions as Lee. While both recognized the possibility, they were not completely sure whether the army could maneuver around the Mexican left. Scott directed them to continue their reconnaissance the next day and detailed to Lee a work party to cut a trail. By the end of that day, Lee and his crew had prepared a passable new trail up the ravine (Freeman, *Lee* 1:241).

Not only was Lee responsible for finding the route and building the road, Scott also entrusted him with serving as guide for Brigadier General David Twiggs's division in the conduct of the attack. Freeman refers to this latter mission as "two days of the heaviest responsibility [Lee] had ever known" (Freeman, *Lee* 1:242). Lee led Twiggs's men up the ravines that passed around Santa Anna's left, emplaced an artillery battery, and guided a brigade around the northern flank of Cerro Gordo with the intention of cutting off the enemy retreat (Freeman, *Lee* 1:242–244).

Lee performed all these tasks with distinction. Scott wrote that Lee was "indefatigable during these operations, in reconnaissance as daring as laborious, and of the utmost value." Lee was brevetted to major "for gallant and meritorious conduct in the battle of Cerro Gordo." Freeman summarizes that "no other officer of the army received such high praise; none gained so much in prestige by the action" (*Lee* 1:247–248).

IMPACT ON LEE

Thus, as an engineer in Mexico, Lee developed the genius for intelligence, reconnaissance, understanding the terrain, and turning the enemy that marked his generalship as commander of the Army of Northern Virginia during the Civil War. Archer Jones writes that "the Mexican War created an informal, unwritten tactical doctrine—to turn the enemy" (271), and Lee was particularly influenced by this development. Burke Davis observes that, whether in Mexico or in Virginia, "Lee, somehow, always found a route to the vulnerable flank of the enemy" (40). Davis's word choice is instructive. Indeed, Lee always found a way to turn the enemy, and he did this through reconnaissance—a skill he had learned in Mexico. Emory Thomas notes that it was in Mexico that Lee learned to "act upon accurate reconnaissance" (*Lee* 140), and Freeman states that it was there that Lee "had disclosed a special aptitude for reconnaissance" (*Lee* 1:246–247). These lessons were borne out in the Civil War, where Freeman concludes that Lee's "offensive strategy rested upon thorough study of the terrain" (S. Smith 168). It was a skill he had learned as an engineer in Mexico.

An excellent example of Lee applying this skill is at Chancellorsville and Stonewall Jackson's famous flank march along a route reconnoitered by Major Jedediah Hotchkiss. Equally telling, however, is how the lack of reconnaissance could negatively affect Lee. The best example of this is at Gettysburg, where Lee was deprived of the services of Jeb Stuart. Freeman writes that Lee "had become dependent upon [Stuart] for information on the enemy's position and plans, and in Stuart's absence, he had no satisfactory form of military intelligence. . . . The injudicious employment of the Confederate horse during the Gettysburg campaign was responsible for most of the other mistakes on the Southern side" (*Lee* 3:147–148).

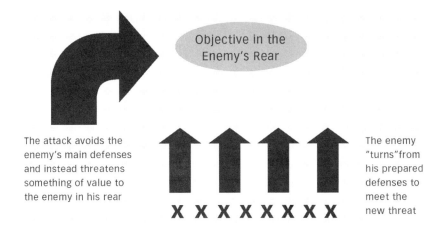

The attack avoids the enemy's main defenses and instead threatens something of value to the enemy in his rear

Objective in the Enemy's Rear

The enemy "turns" from his prepared defenses to meet the new threat

X X X X X X X X

TURNING MOVEMENT

Lee understood the value of reconnaissance, both of the enemy and of the terrain. He had learned in Mexico that such intelligence could be used to turn the enemy—a maneuver that became his favorite. Chancellorsville showed how Lee could use the knowledge of the terrain to develop a tactical plan to gain great advantage over his opponent—just as he had helped Scott to do at Cerro Gordo. Gettysburg showed how dependent Lee had become on such intelligence and how detrimental fighting without it could be.

Pierre Gustave Toutant Beauregard and the Exception that Proves the Rule

As an engineer lieutenant in Mexico, Pierre Gustave Toutant Beauregard had not been shy about expressing his opinion. He attempted to persuade Brigadier General David Twiggs to concentrate all available forces against Cerro Gordo itself, believing that Twiggs's plan to focus instead on the Mexican batteries would work but entailed unnecessary risks. Even more boldly and persuasively, Beauregard provided commentary on General Scott's plan for Chapultepec (J. Eisenhower, *So Far* 276–277, 337–338).

OPINION OF SCOTT

It was not that Beauregard did not admire Scott. Indeed, he thought him "the best general of the day." Still, Beauregard thought that Scott "has not been faultless" and attributed much of Scott's success to the weakness of the Mexicans. Had Scott faced a more worthy opponent, Beauregard thought Scott would have been forced to follow more closely "the true principles of the art of war, on the one or two occasions he departed from and which does not happen with impunity in a well conducted war." While most Mexican War veterans saw Scott's turning movements as proven maneuvers to be emulated, Beauregard was apprehensive. He feared the requirement of dividing the army necessitated by a turning movement, cautioning that "the enemy occupying a central position to our line of operations might then concentrate all his means" against one or the other part. Almost alone among the important Civil War generals, Beauregard would not typically employ the turning movement (Hattaway and Jones 16–17).

An early example of this style is at First Manassas, where Beauregard faced Irvin McDowell, another Mexican War veteran. McDowell's plan called for a turning movement around the Confederate left—the doctrine McDowell had learned in Mexico (Hattaway and Jones 41). True to form, Beauregard was critical of such a plan, calling it a good one only "against a passive defensive opponent" (Beauregard 218), a comment consistent with his conclusion that Scott's tactics in Mexico succeeded only because the Mexicans were such a weak adversary. Beauregard found McDowell's turning movement to result in "a severed movement of [McDowell's] forces," which left McDowell exposed and weak (Beauregard 218). For his part, Beauregard planned to approach the battle in a much more direct way. His plan certainly had some elements of a flank attack, but Hattaway and Jones still describe it as "merely to advance [Beauregard's] strengthened right wing against the Union left" (42). Beauregard's plan certainly showed much less of a turning movement than did McDowell's.

SHILOH

The most notable example of Beauregard's dislike for the turning movement, however, is Shiloh, where Beauregard, although second in command to Albert Sydney Johnston, was responsible for developing the plan of attack and then, after Johnston's death, executing it. In an April 3 memorandum to his corps commanders, Johnston specifically stated that "every effort should be made to turn the left flank of the enemy so as to cut off his line of retreat to the Tennessee River, and throw him back on Owl Creek." Johnston expected to push rapidly with his right wing around the Federal left. Such a move would drive the Federals downstream away from their base of supplies at Pittsburg Landing. The Confederates would then envelop and defeat them (T. Williams, *Beauregard* 177).

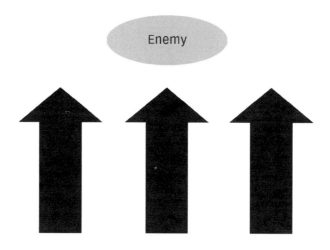

FRONTAL ATTACK

Beauregard, however, deviated from this intent in drafting the actual order for the attack. The result was a frontal attack in which it appeared that Beauregard thought that by a combination of surprise and sheer numbers, he could simply overpower the Federals. He made no provision for placing a large number of troops on the Confederate right as would be required by Johnston's plan. Beauregard appears to have never intended anything but a frontal attack.

As the battle unfolded, Johnston failed to exert his will over Beauregard and try to get a turning force on his right until after the battle was well begun (McDonough 73–75). By then it was too late, and the opportunity was lost. If a large force had been present on the Confederate right when the battle opened and when the Confederates had the advantages of surprise and momentum, the chances are that the Confederates would have broken through as Johnston's original plan envisioned (McDonough 168).

Instead, the actual result was three corps attacking on line, one behind another, each line feeding its components piecemeal into the line ahead (Nevin 128; Foote 1:338). Ulysses S. Grant recalled, "The endeavor of the enemy on the first day was simply to hurl their men against ours—first at one point, then at another, sometimes at several points at once" (190). The frontal assault succeeded responsibly well, but proceeded so slowly that the fighting lasted all

P. G. T. Beauregard. National Archives and
Records Administration.

day long, forfeiting the initial Confederate advantage of surprise (Hattaway
and Jones 168).

Nowhere was this lack of imagination more disastrously apparent than at
the Hornet's Nest. Here Brigadier General Benjamin Prentiss and his division
halted the Confederate advance for several critical hours while the Federal line
elsewhere was given a chance to stabilize. After eleven assaults, the Confederates massed sixty-two artillery pieces and finally, one hour before nightfall,
blasted Prentiss from his stronghold. An estimated 10,000 Confederates had
been thrown into the Hornet's Nest fight. Precious time and lives had been lost
on the frontal assault. A flanking movement would probably have produced
the desired results, but Beauregard and the Confederate command instead relied on brute force rather than on finesse (Daniel 214).

LOST OPPORTUNITY

Archer Jones's conclusion that "the Mexican War created an informal, unwritten tactical doctrine—to turn the enemy" (271) has been challenged by
Grady McWhiney and Perry Jamieson, who argue that many veterans chose
to ignore Mexico's many turning movements and instead concentrate on its

frontal attacks that did succeed (160; Beringer et al. 458). Stephen Carney high-lights this observation for those officers who took their example from Zachary Taylor, who, after a rough start, often succeeded in carrying well-fortified po-sitions. Carney writes, "In that light, many future leaders—such as Grant, George G. Meade, Braxton Bragg, George H. Thomas, and John F. Reyn-olds—came to believe that the offense always held primacy over the defensive. During the Civil War, they would conduct many disasterous [*sic*] frontal as-saults against well-entrenched defenders" (*Gateway* 32). To make their point, however, McWhiney and Jamieson use some incomplete statistics (Beringer et al. 465). Richard Beringer and his colleagues suggest that while some Mexi-can War veterans indeed learned the wrong lesson about frontal attacks, many other factors explain why frontal attacks persisted into the Civil War. Lack of training and experience made the simplicity of the frontal attack invit-ing. Even contempt for the enemy may have motivated some frontal attacks. Beringer and his colleagues allow that "many factors must have contributed to the number of ill-advised frontal attacks" (473), but to explain Beauregard's situation, one must return to Jones's observation.

What failed to impress upon Beauregard the lesson of the turning move-ment was exactly its "informal" and "unwritten" nature that Jones describes. Indeed, T. Harry Williams assesses that "much of Scott's brilliant strategy was lost on Beauregard because it did not come out of the books." For Beauregard, warfare was to be waged according to a fairly rigid set of rules in conformity to a fixed pattern. Scott's bold departure from some of Beauregard's cherished rules shocked him, and he could not accept the risks associated with such au-dacity. Williams concludes that "there is no evidence that [Beauregard] studied Scott's generalship in the Mexican campaign or learned anything from the general's strategy, as Lee undoubtedly did. . . . Here was Beauregard's greatest weakness as a soldier. . . . He could not easily adjust his thinking to an actual situation or improvise new ways of war. Too many times he would go by the rules in the book" (*Beauregard* 52).

Generations of Confederate sympathizers have lamented the "lost oppor-tunity" of Shiloh, blaming Beauregard for a series of blunders without which the Federal army might have been destroyed (McDonough 168). In reality, the lost opportunity for Beauregard occurred not in the decisions he made on the battlefield of Shiloh but in the lessons he failed to learn from his service in Mexico.

Jefferson Davis and Misplaced Confidence

T. Harry Williams writes that "if modern computer-calculators had been available in 1861, they would have surely forecast that Jefferson Davis would be a great war director and Abraham Lincoln an indifferent one" (*History* 248). Lincoln's only firsthand experience with military service was during the Black Hawk War in 1832, in which he joined and rejoined the militia three times, serving a total of eighty days and experiencing no combat action at all (Hattaway and Jones 3). Davis, on the other hand, had graduated from West Point in 1828, served as a regimental commander in the Mexican War, and been secretary of war under President Franklin Pierce. Herman Hattaway and Archer Jones conclude that "Davis's breadth of background probably better qualified him for high army command than any man in the United States." They continue, however, cautioning that "yet some of Davis's background would also be a handicap" (Hattaway and Jones 9). Part of this handicap can be traced to Davis's experience in the Mexican War.

BUENA VISTA

After graduating from West Point, Davis served seven years on the northwest frontier, resigning in 1835 as a first lieutenant. He settled down to a life as a Mississippi planter until 1845, when he was elected to Congress. When the Mexican War broke out, Davis left Congress in order to enlist. He was selected to command the Mississippi Rifles, a volunteer regiment. As such, Davis fell under the command of Brigadier General Zachary Taylor, the father of Davis's first wife, Knox, who had died just three months after their marriage.

February 1847 found Taylor possessing excellent defensive ground, guarding the approaches to Buena Vista but facing a numerically superior army and
being unsure of Santa Anna's intentions. Taylor himself was located six miles
north of Buena Vista at the more vulnerable Saltillo. Arrangement of the defense of Buena Vista fell to Brigadier General John Wool. Wool had identi-
fied three avenues of approach available to Santa Anna. He defended the most
likely approach, the main Saltillo–San Luis Potosi road, and the most dangerous, a broad plain east of the road known as the Plateau. The third avenue
was a relatively narrow ridge that led around Wool's east flank straight to
Buena Vista in the American's rear. For the moment, Wool was willing to accept risk along this avenue, and he did not immediately protect it (J. Eisenhower, *So Far* 184–185).

On the morning of February 22, Taylor concluded that nothing significant would happen at Saltillo, and he departed for Buena Vista. He arrived at
Wool's position around 11:00 A.M. By 3:00 P.M., the battle had begun.

Santa Anna had both attacked in the center and discovered the unprotected
avenue on the American's east flank. Taylor ordered forward two regiments of
Arkansas and Kentucky cavalry and a battalion of Indiana infantry and, after
some small fighting and adjustments to the line, was confident the position was
strong. Still concerned about his vulnerable rear, Taylor returned that night to
Saltillo to supervise operations there.

Early the next morning, Santa Anna attacked in force. When Taylor returned on the scene at about 9:00 A.M., success appeared to be within Santa
Anna's grasp. Wool reported, "General, we are whipped," to which Taylor replied, "That is for me to determine" (J. Eisenhower, *So Far* 187–188).

Davis's Mississippi Rifles had ridden forward from Saltillo with Taylor,
and now Taylor ordered them to rally the fleeing Second Indiana and hold the
faltering east flank. The Mississippians and other reinforcements were able to
halt the Mexican advance.

At this point, Santa Anna decided to send his uncommitted division along
the third avenue of approach on the extreme American east flank. Taylor detected this move and immediately sent Davis's Mississippi Rifles and the Third
Indiana to intercept it. Davis positioned the two regiments in an unorthodox
but highly effective inverted V formation on top of a ridge overlooking the
Mexican approach. There he waited until the enemy reached a point just sev-

FLIGHT OF THE MEXICAN ARMY.
AT THE BATTLE OF BUENA VISTA FEB' 23. 1847.

Library of Congress, Prints and Photographs Reading Room, reproduction number LC-USZ62-93028 (b&w film copy neg.).

enty yards away and opened fire all at once. The Mexican advance dissolved, and the Mississippians descended on the remnants with their bowie knives. Only a sudden thunderstorm saved the Mexicans from even greater destruction (J. Eisenhower, *So Far* 189).

Buena Vista had proved to be a close call for Taylor, but when the sun came up on February 24, the Americans found Santa Anna had withdrawn during the night. Davis deserved his share of the credit for his aggressive and innovative tactics. Indeed, even the Duke of Wellington took notice of Davis's exploits (Canfield 29).

Others, too, were impressed by Davis's performance in Mexico. In 1847, he was offered, but declined, an appointment as brigadier general in the U.S. Army, returning instead to his political career. But among those who saw greatness in Davis's deeds in Mexico was Davis himself, and this would come back to haunt the Confederacy when Davis became its president. As Davis's biographer Cass Canfield concludes, "Buena Vista was a relatively minor battle, so that the young colonel should not have assumed, as he did, that he was expert as a tactician and strategist. This assumption led to overconfidence when Davis was called upon to direct the military effort of the Confederacy" (29–30). Indeed, near the close of the Civil War, the *Richmond Examiner*, recalling the consequences of the chain of events that resulted from Davis's success at Buena Vista, lamented, "If we are to perish, the verdict of posterity will be, 'Died of a V'" (McWhiney, "Davis" 101).

In addition to gaining great confidence in his own abilities thanks to Buena Vista, Davis also had a very self-reliant role model in Zachary Taylor. Unlike Scott, who made maximum use of his staff, especially his engineers, Taylor minimized preliminary reconnaissance, had little use for intelligence, and kept his quartermaster uninformed (Bauer 34; T. Williams, *History* 165). While Scott's "little cabinet" of West Pointers comprised "the first American field army staff to approach adequacy," Taylor's forte remained individual command rather than collective staff effort (Weigley, *History* 181, 185). Davis's confidence in his own abilities was reinforced by the command style he learned under Taylor. Davis would command the same self-reliant way in the Civil War.

PRESIDENT OF THE CONFEDERATE STATES OF AMERICA

With this attitude of self-confidence and superiority, Davis took his title as commander in chief of the Confederate army quite literally. Indeed, Chris Fonvielle assesses that Davis "considered himself a military leader first and a politician second" (49). Although he had six secretaries of war in four years, for all practical purposes Davis served as his own secretary of war and chief of staff. Clifford Dowdey observes that "as everything about the military fascinated him and he believed only he was capable of running things, the President performed tasks that belonged properly to clerks in the War Office, and even in the Adjutant General's office. Conversely, as he squandered his time and energies in the field of his interests, Davis neglected affairs which properly belonged in the President's office" (*Land* 128). Emory Thomas agrees that Davis "considered his military experience and instincts the most important contributions he could offer his new nation" (*Lee* 198). To be fair, there are a few contrarian theories. Admitting he is "tread[ing] the borders of the realm of speculation," Steven Woodworth suggests Davis's real problem was "a basic insecurity," which prevented him from overcoming all other failings (316). Woodworth notwithstanding, the preponderance of evidence and analysis concludes that Davis believed he had skills and experience sufficient to act as commander in chief without needing much help. Davis's energies were misplaced, however, and the Confederate nation suffered for it.

Buena Vista and his other military experiences had given Davis such confidence in his own capabilities that he denied himself the advice and counsel of others. At the beginning of the Civil War, the military structure of the Confederacy mirrored that of the United States, with the exception that there was no provision for a general in chief. In early 1862, Davis asked Congress to authorize the position, not because Davis thought he needed help but because he thought such an appointment would quiet some of his critics. When Congress voted to establish the position, Davis, having decided it would infringe upon his powers as commander in chief, vetoed the legislation.

Still hoping to put in place some buffer between the War Department and Congress, Davis used his own authority to create the office of general in chief in March. He named General Robert E. Lee to the post, charging him "under the direction of the President with the conduct of military operations in the armies of the Confederacy" (T. Williams, *History* 254).

In Davis's mind, the phrase "under the direction of the President" was key to his concept of Lee's authority. Essentially, Lee was limited to acting as a provider of counsel and information, with no authority to initiate or direct any large strategic operations (T. Williams, *History* 254). Lee's biographer Douglas Southall Freeman calls it "an impossible assignment" and concludes that in Lee's "whole career there was not a period of more thankless service" (*Lee* 2:1–7).

Lee vacated the position in June to assume field command of the Army of Northern Virginia, and Davis left the adviser position vacant for approximately twenty months, an indication of how little importance he attached to the office. During that time, Davis formulated strategy largely without professional advice. The proximity of Lee to Davis in the eastern theater helped facilitate strategic planning there, but operations in the western theater suffered greatly (Nevin 36).

In February 1864, Davis finally revived the position, filling it with Braxton

Bragg. Bragg's field command in the West had resulted in disaster, and Davis had been forced by public opinion to remove him. But Bragg was a personal friend and a pliable tool, exactly what Davis desired for the adviser position. Bragg understood his role and restricted his function to gratuitous advice and sycophantic praise.

With any realistic chances of Confederate victory a thing of the past, Congress created the office of general in chief in February 1865, and Davis finally appointed Lee to the position. Even then Davis emphasized in his directive that he was still commander in chief. With merely two months remaining in the war, the new arrangement died without being fairly tested (T. Williams, *History* 255).

Jefferson Davis was an extremely capable man. Thoughtful reviewers such as Archer Jones have concluded that "he seems to have had fewer defects as military commander and strategist than many historians have found in him and displayed more insight and ability than they have noted" (223). Indeed, Davis's chief defect appears to have been one of character rather than capability. He was too confident in his own abilities, and much of the confidence stemmed from Mexico. In many ways, it defined him. Even after the Civil War, in a debate over some military matter, Davis defended the correctness of his position based on his Mexican War "experience as a commander of volunteers" (McWhiney, "Davis" 112).

The Bible cautions, "For by wise counsel thou shalt make thy war; and in multitude of counselors there is safety" (Proverbs 24:6). Davis failed to heed this advice, instead placing excessive reliance on his own experience, experience he had thought he gained in Mexico.

BRAXTON BRAGG AND
JEFFERSON DAVIS

With Jefferson Davis at Buena Vista was Braxton Bragg, commanding a battery of artillery. Bragg would go on to be a full general in the Confederate Army, commanding the Army of Tennessee. It would be a tumultuous and controversial command and one in which the relationship between Bragg and Davis would play a key part. Many would conclude that the confidence Bragg earned from Davis at Buena Vista lasted long after it should have in the Civil War. But while Bragg was able to get along well with Davis, he had a very different effect on his men. In Mexico, the seeds were sown both for Davis's Civil War support of Bragg and for Bragg's Civil War reputation as an unnecessarily harsh authoritarian.

BRAGG AND HIS MEN

Bragg was a rigid disciplinarian in Mexico. He had an enthusiasm for drilling that seemed excessive, and many characterized him as "humorless, exacting and petty . . . dull, sour and pedantic" (Kuehl 55). Most considered him a martinet. Bragg's attention to detail and insistence on precision undoubtedly were critical to his success as an artilleryman, but such an attitude also made him unpopular with many of the rank and file. In October 1847, a report surfaced that a soldier had placed an eight-inch bombshell under Bragg's bed and ignited it. While the explosion was terrific, Bragg escaped unharmed. The account of the incident could offer no explanation for the attempt on Bragg's life "except that some of his men think he is too severe in his discipline. This is the second attempt upon his life" (McWhiney, *Bragg* 97–98).

Bragg would continue this ability to incite passionate vindictiveness among the rank and file in the Civil War. One private wrote, "Breathe softly the name . . . Bragg, it has more terror than the [enemy] army," and "We . . . did not . . . so much love our country, as we feared Bragg" (Hattaway and Jones 315–316).

Daniel Kuehl observes that the army of Zachary Taylor in which Bragg served in Mexico "was in some ways similar to the Confederate army, composed of volunteer soldiers of whom Bragg had been openly contemptuous. Men who distrusted the regular army could be led to greatness by a great leader—this Bragg was not. The attention to minutia and strict discipline that made him a successful battery commander in Mexico were not the traits needed to inspire an Army" (64). But while Bragg's soldiers may not have liked him, his president seems to have.

BRAGG AND DAVIS

Bragg's poor performance in the Kentucky Campaign "caused nearly every Confederate except Davis to lose confidence in Bragg" (McWhiney, *Bragg* 329). His problems continued when, after Chickamauga, a petition signed by such high-ranking officers as James Longstreet, Simon Buckner, Patrick Cleburne, D. H. Hill, Leonidas Polk, and William Preston requested that Davis remove Bragg from command, contending, "[t]he Army of Tennessee, stricken with complete paralysis, may deem itself fortunate if it escapes from its present position without disaster" (Hallock 95–96). The situation was serious enough that Davis himself visited the army to investigate. Cleburne told Davis that Bragg's failures "had totally lost him the confidence of the army, and . . . this fact alone destroyed his usefulness." Longstreet stated that Bragg "could be of greater service elsewhere than at the head of the Army of Tennessee" (Hallock 98–99). Nonetheless, Davis upheld Bragg as commander. Only after the loss of Chattanooga did Davis replace Bragg, and then only after Bragg had asked to be relieved. Even at that, Davis did not turn against Bragg. In February 1864, Davis appointed Bragg as his military adviser, charged with responsibility for "the conduct of military operations in the Armies of the Confederacy" (Hallock 163).

Throughout it all, Davis clearly had a soft spot for Bragg. A newspaper reported, "It is said the President wept when he heard of General Bragg's misfortunes at Lookout Mountain and Missionary Ridge. Certainly the President was very much attached to the General" (Hallock 150).

WHY?

The roots of Davis's attachment to Bragg stem from Buena Vista, where both men earned early and enduring glory. Bragg's batteries, along with those of Major J. M. Washington, were firing with support of the Second Indiana Regiment. The infantry was forced out of line, leaving the artillery to fend for itself. Bragg and Washington did so, falling back in good order, limbering and unlimbering from time to time, and precariously fighting to keep the Mexican assault in check.

Then Davis and his Mississippians came to the artillery's aid. Davis formed his men in what would become the famous V. The Mexicans charged into the open end and were repulsed by fire.

After halting the Mexican advance, Davis's infantry fell back behind the artillery. At this critical moment, Bragg arrived with his battery and reported to Taylor. Taylor either told Bragg the more likely "double-shot your guns and give 'em hell, Bragg" or the more romanticized "a little more grape, Captain Bragg" (Kuehl 62).

Either way, Davis was very impressed by Bragg's performance. He wrote in his report, "After marching two or three hundred yards we saw the enemy's infantry advancing in three lines upon Bragg's battery, which, though entirely unsupported, resolutely held its position and met the attack with a fire worthy of the former achievements of the battery, and the reputation of its meritorious commander" (Seitz 10) Kuehl writes, "Earlier, Bragg had arrived in the nick of time to help Davis, and had admired the way the Mississippian coolly held his ground. Now it was Davis's turn to arrive just in time to help Bragg, and to note Bragg's steadiness in the face of the enemy" (62). Indeed, one explanation of why Davis was so tolerant of Bragg's Civil War shortcomings

"A little more grape Captain Bragg." General Zachary Taylor at the battle of Buena Vista, February 23, 1847. Lithograph by N. Currier, 1847. Library of Congress, Prints and Photographs Reading Room, reproduction number LC-USZC2-2774.

could certainly be that Davis chose to recall this Mexican War memory whenever he saw Bragg.

Others disagree. Bragg's early biographer Don Seitz thought that "the part played by [Bragg] in association with Jefferson Davis in the Mexican War had bred an intimacy that received undue credit in after years, as the basis for the latter's strong support of Bragg in the presence of what were deemed military inadequacies" (14). Archer Jones acknowledges Davis's "clinging to Bragg" but explains it as part of Davis's greater "reluctance to relieve commanders" (221, 222). Davis himself told Bragg in 1872 that he did not relieve Bragg because Davis was convinced "no change for the better could be made in the commander of the army." Judith Hallock interprets this to mean that Davis believed he had no alternative to Bragg (99).

In the final analysis, it is clear that Davis's positive experience with Bragg in Mexico influenced his decision making regarding Bragg in the Civil War. If Davis truly thought that the Army of Tennessee was best served by Bragg, then why did Davis eventually succumb and replace Bragg with Joe Johnston, certainly no favorite of Davis's? Davis gave Bragg every possible opportunity and support as commander, relieved him only when Bragg requested it, and then continued to sponsor Bragg by making him his military adviser. Steven Woodworth notes that one of Davis's tragic flaws was that "he could not see the faults of his friends" (305), and this was certainly the case with Bragg. Woodworth definitively states, "Bragg was Davis's general" (309), and clearly Davis had a special affection for Bragg that would weather many storms. It was the kind of lasting affection that could best be earned on a distant battlefield during better times.

JOHN WINDER AND
WARTIME GOVERNANCE

John Winder demonstrated remarkable coolness and bravery under fire in the Mexican War and was brevetted to lieutenant colonel for his meritorious conduct at Chapultepec and Mexico City. However, his most important experience in Mexico, so far as his later Civil War career would be concerned, was his service as lieutenant governor of Vera Cruz. During the Civil War, Winder would serve as provost marshal general of Richmond. His biographer Arch Blakely notes, "Winder gained much experience in Vera Cruz that he would later need in governing Richmond, but not all of that experience was transferable to another situation. . . . He learned then, probably to his great dismay, that he could not treat Richmonders as defeated subjects or trample their cherished freedoms with impunity, as he was able to do in Vera Cruz" (104–105).

VERA CRUZ

With the conquest of Mexico City, fighting virtually ended, and a military occupation of Mexico began. Twelve cities were placed under martial law and garrisoned with American troops until August 1848. Winder was ordered to Vera Cruz on December 9, 1847, and became the city's lieutenant governor.

Winder was charged with keeping the peace and was given the necessary authority and resources to do so. He had two companies under his direct control and three more at his disposal if needed. In addition to functioning as chief of police, Winder presided over military courts and dispensed the punishments the courts ordered. He superintended jails, attending to the needs of prisoners, arranging for guards, and establishing watches (Blakely 104).

Winder was intensely involved in disciplinary actions. There were many fights between civilians and soldiers, and Winder meted out stiff punishments, including confinement, flogging, hard labor, and death. Other of Winder's duties involved issuing gambling licenses, returning captured runaway slaves, and censoring the press (Blakely 104).

Winder's duty as lieutenant governor ended with the signing of the peace treaty on July 29, 1848, and on August 1 he sailed back to the United States with his unit. In Vera Cruz, Winder had been "firm but fair, and his rule was effective" (Blakely 104). Still, his experience in Mexico was unique. The Mexican people under his control no doubt resented the American presence, but they were generally docile in accepting it. Winder was "operating in a conquered country with the full force of the military behind him." His power was immense. If he thought the press was out of line, he censored the offending material or shut the entire publication down. If civilians became restless, he had sufficient force to restore the peace. Winder excelled as military governor at Vera Cruz because his actions were subjected to very few limitations. Blakely assesses that at Vera Cruz, Winder "proved conclusively that he could control a captive people and unruly soldiers, but this was not the situation he faced during the Civil War" (105). Richmond would be a different experience for Winder, and the transition would not be altogether a smooth one. There Winder would be in his own homeland trying to control his fellow countrymen.

RICHMOND

On March 1, 1862, President Jefferson Davis declared martial law in Richmond, appointed Winder provost marshal general, and ordered him to establish an efficient police system within a ten-mile radius of the city (Blakely 119). Winder's task was a delicate one. Especially in the South, Americans had a strong notion of individual rights. In fact, resistance to the central government had been the very reason the Confederate states had seceded from the Union. Throughout the war, all Confederate attempts to centralize control at the expense of individual liberties would be viewed with suspicion and resistance. Indeed, David Donald argues that the epitaph of the Confederacy should be "Died of Democracy" (90). Richmond would prove a difficult challenge for Winder.

One of the first activities Winder sought to control was the consumption of alcohol. In the process, he resorted to entrapping druggists honoring forged prescriptions for medicinal alcohol. As part of the operation, several of Winder's detectives, whom Clifford Dowdey describes as "bully boys" and "imported plug-uglies" (*Land* 183), were caught consuming the evidence. The ensuing controversy weakened Winder's credibility, especially when he mistakenly supported many of his detectives who in fact had acted improperly (Blakely 123–124).

Winder also had a complicated relationship with the press. While freedom of the press was seriously abridged in the North, little was done to curb free expression in the South (Donald 87). Indeed, Robert E. Lee complained that from the tone of the press, it would appear the Confederacy had "put all our worst generals to commanding our armies, and all our best generals to editing newspapers" (Donald 85). But if Confederate leaders could tolerate editorial criticism, a more dangerous threat was the value of newspapers as a source of intelligence to the enemy (Feis 200). The situation reached the point that Secretary of War Judah Benjamin ordered the press to abstain from any mention of the arrival of arms or other matériel from overseas. A controversy followed surrounding fear that Winder would use Benjamin's declaration to impose a "reign of terror" aimed at the press. Such a reign never materialized, and, compared to the more than 13,000 people who were arbitrarily arrested and some 300 newspapers that were at least temporarily suppressed in the North, Winder's efforts to control the press were a minor irritant at best (Blakely 127–129).

More serious were complaints against Winder's policy of price controls. In an attempt to limit exorbitant prices, Winder established a maximum price for most commodities. If violations occurred, both buyer and seller would be court-martialed, and the informer would be given the produce. Soon both honest and dishonest people were afraid to do business in Richmond. Food supplies almost disappeared, and many citizens left Richmond in search of food. Eventually, Winder bowed to pressure and lifted the price controls, but prices

Libby Prison was one of John Winder's responsibilities in Richmond.
Library of Congress, Prints and Photographs Division, reproduction
number LC-B8171-3364 DLC (b&w film copy neg.).

soared, and he later reimposed the controls on corn, livestock fodder, and straw.
Results were inconsistent, and Winder was spared further trouble arriving at
the proper solution when the War Department declared that martial law did
not include price-fixing (Blakely 129–130).

Winder's role in the daily life of Richmond touched nearly every detail. He
broke strikes, fixed newspaper prices, rounded up spies, registered foreigners,
returned deserters to the ranks, enforced conscription, managed prisons, and
guarded key facilities (Blakely 131–138). Dowdey describes Winder's command
as "combining the functions of MPs, the FBI, and the Border Patrol" (*Land*
183). Winder remained in his position in Richmond until May 25, 1863, when
he was reassigned to Goldsboro, North Carolina, to become the commander
of the state's Second District. His tenure as provost marshal of Richmond
had been difficult and controversial. He had usually been effective, but not
always popular. Even his critics conceded he got results. According to one

observer, Winder cleaned out Richmond "from center to circumference. Spies, traitors, loafers, slackers, all were swept out, saloons and gambling houses were closed . . . in short, order was brought out of chaos" (Blakely 121).

But the issue was not with Winder's results. It was with his methods. Blakely concludes that in Richmond, "[f]ew would argue with the goals [Winder] espoused, but many would disagree with the means he employed to the end" (118). Dowdey would agree, characterizing Winder as "unloved" (*Land* 183).

Richmond was simply a different situation than Winder had encountered in Vera Cruz, where there was no need to persuade, accommodate, or placate the citizenry. In Mexico, Winder learned how to efficiently and authoritatively impose order on a conquered people. Criticism of his later efforts in Richmond suggests he relied on the same heavy-handed tactics from Mexico, which were not as appropriate amid a friendly population who greatly valued their democratic liberties. For failing to make this adjustment, many remember Winder as the "dictator of Richmond" (Blakely 119).

John Slidell and
Doomed Diplomacy

One area in common between the Mexican War and Civil War was the inability to resolve the conflict through diplomacy. John Slidell would play a key part in both of these futile efforts. In Mexico, Slidell would land at Vera Cruz on November 29, 1845, as America's minister-delegate with what John Eisenhower describes as "an impossible task" (*So Far* 45). On May 8, 1846, Slidell would return to the United States, his mission a failure. But the failure did not mean nothing was gained. Slidell's biographer Louis Sears notes that in Mexico, "Slidell had broadened an experience which was later to bring him forward as the foremost diplomat of the Confederate States and to secure for him the post of minister to France" (73). However, that mission as well would be doomed to failure.

AN IMPOSSIBLE TASK

From the moment Slidell landed at Vera Cruz, his mission was tense. Earlier, on October 13, Mexican foreign minister Manuel Pena y Pena announced that he would receive Slidell only as a "commissioner" rather than as a full-fledged "minister." The Mexicans' position reflected their assessment of the illegitimacy of American actions. Mexico perceived the annexation of Texas as a casus belli. Acceptance of a minister implied restoration of normalized relations, which would permit opponents of General Jose Herrera's government to charge acceptance of the loss of Texas. Such a challenge would likely topple Herrera's already weakened government (Bauer 25).

To make maters worse, the American position left Slidell little with which to assuage the Mexicans. Slidell was instructed to offer no reparation for annexing Texas, to reference the "injuries and outrages committed by . . . Mexico on American citizens," and to offer four alternative boundary adjustments in lieu of monetary reparations. It all amounted to what Eisenhower calls "a neat shopping list" (*So Far* 45–46).

Slidell did not get to advance his demands anytime soon. He reached Mexico City on December 6, but the Mexicans refused to meet with him as long as he insisted on the title of "minister." Infuriated, Slidell left Mexico City for Jalapa to await further instructions from Washington. As he departed, he unfurled a series of insinuations of Mexican bad faith, designed obviously to build the case for future intervention. In early January 1846, Slidell notified President Polk that he had given up hope of reaching a settlement. Diplomacy had failed, and on January 13 Secretary of War William Marcy notified Zachary Taylor in Corpus Christi, "Sir: I am directed by the President to instruct you to advance and occupy, with the troops under your command, positions on or near the east bank of the Rio del Norte" (J. Eisenhower, *So Far* 47–48).

Some halting efforts to resolve the matter diplomatically continued, including a scheme to buy out the Mexicans for $30 million, but in April Slidell ended his efforts, notifying Polk the Mexicans would not receive him (J. Eisenhower, *So Far* 60). By May 8, Slidell was back in Washington, arguing that the time for talk was over and that Polk should now "act with promptness and energy" using military means (J. Eisenhower, *So Far* 66). By May 12, both the House and the Senate had voted to approve Polk's recommendation for war.

LITTLE HOPE AGAIN

After Mexico, Slidell served as a senator from Louisiana, enjoyed personal prestige during the Buchanan administration, and cast his lot with Louisiana when the state decided to secede. By then he had earned a national reputation, and in the late summer of 1861 President Davis appointed him to the post of commissioner to France. In early February 1862, after a most eventful transatlantic voyage, Slidell arrived in Paris.

As in Mexico, Slidell did not find a warm welcome to greet him. He received a cool reception from M. Thouvenel, French minister of foreign affairs, and found Thouvenel's denial of France's consultations with Great Britain about the blockade disingenuous (L. Sears 187). This was no small matter. Indeed, Great Britain's position would be the key to France's position. Everywhere Slidell turned he found a stubborn refusal on France's part to act on the Confederacy's behalf before Great Britain did. In fact, Slidell concluded that the main Confederate diplomatic effort should be in London, not Paris (L. Sears 188–189, 195).

Slidell's unfulfilled hope for European intervention as a result of Lee's repulse of McClellan's Peninsula Campaign was rekindled when Lee invaded Maryland (L. Sears 203). Prime Minister Lord Palmerston wrote Lord John Russell, British secretary of state for foreign affairs, on September 14, 1862, concerning "an arrangement upon the basis of separation." Russell responded, "I agree with you that the time is come for offering mediation to the United States Government, with a view of the recognition of the Independence of the Confederates—I agree further that in case of failure, we ought ourselves to recognize the Southern States, as an Independent State" (Thomas, *Confederate Nation* 179).

But just as quickly as this energy had gathered, it diffused. Lee was repulsed at Antietam, but that was not the worst of it. President Lincoln took the opportunity on September 22 to issue the Emancipation Proclamation. There was now a moral dimension in the Civil War, and Great Britain, which had emancipated its slaves in 1833, could not be on the wrong side. Thus in October the British cabinet rejected a proposal that England, France, and Russia would intervene in the war and bring about an armistice, a development that would no doubt lead to eventual Confederate independence.

This should have come as no surprise to Slidell and his colleagues. After traveling a year abroad, Confederate politician William Yancey observed, "the feeling against slavery in England is so strong that no public man there dares extend a hand to help us. . . . There is no government in Europe that dares help us in a struggle which can be suspected of having for its result, directly or indirectly, the fortification or perpetuation of slavery. Of that I am certain" (Willson 102). As Bruce Catton observes, after the Emancipation Proclamation, "a pro-Confederate in England now was an apologist for slavery" (*Lincoln's Army* 322).

In spite of this reality, Slidell remained true to his mission. However, not unpredictably, little progress would be made. As late as March 5, 1865, Slidell had an interview with Napoleon III and lamented, "My interview with the Emperor resulted as I supposed it would. He is willing and anxious to act with England but will not move without her" (L. Sears 224). On April 26, Slidell confided to James Mason, the Confederate minister to Great Britain, "[W]e have seen the beginning of the end. I for my part am prepared for the worst" (L. Sears 225). Slidell, of course, was correct. After the war, he remained in exile in France and in Great Britain, where he died in 1871.

FOREGONE CONCLUSIONS

Mexican War historian K. Jack Bauer concludes, "Any knowledgeable observer could have predicted that the Slidell mission would end in failure. It was so ordained by the realities of Mexican domestic politics" (28). One might draw a similar conclusion about Slidell's Civil War efforts. This time Slidell's nemesis would be British domestic politics. The Emancipation Proclamation made British support of the Confederacy untenable. With this development, Slidell's mission in France would be impossible. As a letter addressed to Slidell from "twelve French Patriots of Touis" explained in 1864, "It may be our interest to support you. There may be strong material and political reasons for a close alliance between us, but as long as you maintain and are maintained by slavery we cannot offer you our alliance, but on the contrary, we hope and expect you will fail" (Willson 288). As in Mexico, against such odds, there was little Slidell could do.

GIDEON PILLOW AND POLITICAL GENERALS

As the Civil War began, the U.S. Army rolls included virtually no general officers fit for arduous duty in the field. The rapid expansion of both the Federal and Confederate armies forced Presidents Abraham Lincoln and Jefferson Davis to appoint large numbers of generals. In 1861, Lincoln commissioned 126 generals and Davis 89. Sixty-five percent of those appointed by Lincoln and 50 percent of those appointed by Davis were professional soldiers. The others, 44 Federal generals and 45 Confederate generals, were often appointed for political reasons (Hattaway and Jones 29). Federal Major General Henry Halleck captured the opinion of many professional officers when he wrote of the non-professionals, "It seems but little better than murder to give important commands to such men" (Millett and Maslowski 173).

POLITICAL CONNECTIONS

One political general who served in both the Mexican War and the Civil War and certainly confirmed Halleck's assessment was Gideon Pillow. Disdain for Pillow is almost universal. In the Mexican War, both T. Harry Williams and Russell Weigley agree that Pillow was the very worst of the political generals (T. Williams, *History* 164; Weigley, *History* 175). Bruce Catton assesses that in the Civil War, Pillow "was to bear one distinction, and only one, out of the Civil War—he was the only Confederate general to whom Grant consistently referred in terms of contempt" (*Hallowed* 97).

One of the common criticisms leveled against President James Polk's tenure of office during the Mexican War is his politicizing of the war. Weigley describes Polk as "so zealously partisan a Democrat that he could hardly abide the Whiggery of his two principal generals, Scott and Taylor." As a counter, Polk proposed to Congress the revival of the rank of lieutenant general so that Senator Thomas Hart Benton, a Democrat, might fill it. Weigley writes, "Frustrated in that design, [Polk] did impose upon the Army a dubious set of political commanders of brigades and divisions" (Weigley, *History* 175). One of these was Gideon Pillow.

Pillow was born in 1806 in Tennessee, and he graduated from the University of Nashville. He embarked on a career as a criminal lawyer, and his law partner was none other than James Polk. Ultimately, Pillow became a powerful figure in Democratic politics (Boatner 653–654). Indeed, Pillow's efforts secured Polk's Democratic presidential nomination in Baltimore in 1844 (J. Eisenhower, *So Far* 110).

Pillow had long been a brigadier in the Tennessee militia, but that rank had been political and social only. He had no active military service, and John Eisenhower assesses that "as a soldier, Pillow had little to offer" (*So Far* 111). Nonetheless, his connection to President Polk netted him an appointment as brigadier general in September 1846. This combination of political connection and lack of military experience is not uncommon among political generals in any war, but Eisenhower notes a singularly "menacing aspect to [Pillow]: his role as President Polk's secret informant" (*So Far* 111).

Polk was dissatisfied with his communications with Taylor and Scott, complaining of a "want of reliable information." Polk wrote that Taylor "gives but little information. . . . He seems to act like a regular soldier, whose only duty is to obey orders" and "seems disposed to avoid all responsibility of making any suggestions or giving any opinions." Concerning Scott, Polk thought that he was "no aid to the department" (Henry, *Mexican War* 159). As a counterbalance, Pillow viewed himself as Polk's "representative" in the army (J. Eisenhower, *Agent* 254), and others generally acknowledged him to be "the president's eyes and ears" (Stokes 46). Political intrigue, as well as military ineptitude, would mark Pillow's service in Mexico.

CERRO GORDO

Pillow's first debacle would occur at Cerro Gordo. There Pillow was to provide a secondary attack in support of Brigadier General David Twiggs's main effort. He was to march early in the morning along a route he had previously reconnoitered with Lieutenant Zealous Tower, attack near the Rio del Plan, then turn "right or left, or both" to attack the rear of the three Mexican artillery batteries guarding the National Road (J. Eisenhower, *So Far* 279).

Pillow was no fighter, and he protested these orders from the start, calling his mission a "desperate undertaking." When Scott tried to reassure Pillow that he was not alone—that he was not to attack until he heard firing from Cerro Gordo, at which time the entire Mexican line should collapse—Pillow was unmoved. In a burst of drama, he declared that as a soldier, he would follow Scott's orders even if "he left his bones there." In this state of excitement, Pillow would not budge from the meeting until Scott subtly mentioned the word "discipline." After that, Pillow stalked out (J. Eisenhower, *So Far* 281).

Pillow's apprehension and ineptitude were borne out as soon as the mission began. He abandoned the reconnoitered route and instead led his two regiments along a path visible to the Mexican batteries. To make matters worse, Pillow's shouting at one of his regimental commanders alerted the unsuspecting Mexicans. In the confusion that followed, Pillow received a minor wound in the arm and left the field (J. Eisenhower, *So Far* 255–256). One Pennsylvania volunteer wrote that Pillow "was seen going down the hill in our rear, and was no more seen or heard until the whole engagement was over. . . . The question now is asked, where was . . . Pillow during the heavy firing? . . . Echo answers, where?" (J. Eisenhower, *So Far* 282).

MORE PROBLEMS

Pillow's second debacle stemmed from his actions at and after Chapultepec. Pillow had little involvement in the fighting. He had received a minor wound to his ankle and was dragged to safety early in the battle (J. Eisenhower, *So Far* 295). His real troubles began shortly after the victorious Americans entered

SELF-INFLATING PILLOW.

An 1848 cartoon depicting Gideon Pillow's reputation for self-promotion. Library of Congress, Prints and Photographs Division, reproduction number LC-USZ62-11404 (b&w film copy neg.).

Mexico City. One of the two Mexican howitzers captured at Chapultepec came up missing from Scott's inventory of captured weapons, and it was found in Pillow's baggage wagon.

Pillow tried to get rid of the howitzer, but before he could do so, court-martial charges were preferred against him. He tried unsuccessfully to shift the blame to two young lieutenants and was reprimanded on October 27, 1847. The court agreed that Pillow had in fact returned the souvenir but found that he did so only after he had been discovered. President Polk immediately counter-manded the ruling.

The controversy surrounding Pillow, however, was far from finished. Both in his official report of Conterras and in an anonymous article, obviously initiated by Pillow, that was printed in the *American Star* and the *New Orleans Delta*, Pillow claimed that he had been in command of the army and relegated Scott to an insignificant role. In the ensuing melee, Scott placed Pillow and two other officers under arrest pending a court-martial, but again Polk intervened. He reduced the investigation of Pillow to a court of inquiry, a procedure that bore no criminal implications.

In a politically and emotionally charged court, Pillow, bolstered by his knowledge of Polk's support, displayed his aggressive courtroom oratory and interrogatory skills. In the end, Pillow triumphed, with the court terming his conduct at Conterras "meritorious." John Eisenhower, however, notes Pillow won "not from the strength of [his] case but through the sheer manipulation of governmental power" (*So Far* 320). In his *Memoirs*, Scott describes Pillow as "an anomaly—without the least malignity in his nature—amiable, and possessed of some acuteness, but the only person I have ever known who was wholly indifferent in the choice between truth and falsehood, honesty and dishonesty— ever as ready to attain an end by the one as the other, and habitually boastful of acts of cleverness at the total sacrifice of moral character" (2:416). Pillow celebrated his acquittal at a White House dinner with his friend President Polk.

BETWEEN WARS

One reason Pillow was so jealous of his military reputation was that it facilitated his political aspirations. He hoped to parlay his Mexican War service and his affiliation with Polk into winning the 1852 Democratic presidential nomination. In the summer of 1851, Pillow joined with a group of prominent Democrats, to include Jefferson Davis, to help find a candidate. Secretly, Pillow was working to secure the nomination for himself. Eventually, however, he agreed to work on behalf of Franklin Pierce, who had served in Pillow's division in Mexico and who ultimately won the nomination and the presidency. What Pillow stood to gain from his support of Pierce is unclear, but he was no doubt disappointed when the vice presidential nomination went not to him but to William Rufus King (J. Eisenhower, *Agent* 325–326).

Thwarted in his highest political aspiration, Pillow continued to be an influential Stephen Douglas Democrat. He always maintained his military ties, and when the Civil War broke out, he was appointed the senior major general of Tennessee state troops. His militia forces were subsequently transferred to the Confederate army, and he was chagrined not to be in command of them. He was appointed brigadier general in the Confederate army on July 9, 1861 (Boatner 654).

FORT DONELSON

In February 1862, Pillow found himself second in command at Fort Donelson, Kentucky. The ranking officer there was another political general, John Floyd, who was a former governor of Virginia and secretary of war under President James Buchanan. It was a poor combination. Allan Nevins describes Floyd as a "muddleheaded incompetent" and Pillow as a "vain, hot-tempered [man who] fancied that his reputation as lawyer, planter, and politician, with two Mexican War wounds, made him a general." Third in command was Simon Bolivar Buckner, a competent West Pointer who Nevins says "alone [of the trio] could be taken seriously" (6:22). Indeed, the two politicians would leave Buckner holding the bag at Fort Donelson.

After capturing Fort Henry, Grant moved to Fort Donelson and invested it on February 12, 1862. Grant had nothing but contempt for Floyd and Pillow. In his *Memoirs*, Grant writes Floyd "was no soldier, and I judged that he would yield to Pillow's pretensions." As for Pillow, Grant reports he "had known General Pillow in Mexico, and judged that with any force, no matter how small, I could march up to within gunshot of any intrenchments he was given to hold. I said this to the officers of my staff at the time" (151).

Pillow had not demonstrated an excess of personal bravery when he withdrew from the field after minor wounds on two occasions in Mexico. His behavior at Fort Donelson would continue this pattern.

The Confederates had attempted to break out of their position on February 15 but failed. Floyd then held a council of war with Pillow and Buckner. Floyd and Buckner believed surrender was necessary. Pillow thought the Confederates could hold out another day in the hope of reinforcements or should at least attempt to cut their way out. But Pillow's bellicosity had much more to do with personal safety than devotion to duty. Pillow was most adamant about not surrendering himself. He told Floyd, who as secretary of war had been accused of stocking Southern arsenals with war matériel before the war so that Confederate authorities could seize it when hostilities began, "that he thought there were no two persons in the Confederacy whom the Yankees would prefer to capture than himself and General Floyd" (Henry, "Forrest" 58).

Thus began a strange transfer of command, in which Floyd turned to Pillow and said, "I turn the command over, sir."

"I pass it," Pillow replied promptly.

"I assume it," said Buckner. "Give me pen, ink, and paper, and send for a bugler." As Buckner prepared to surrender, Floyd and Pillow made their escape.

Buckner and Grant were old friends. After the surrender they shared jokes about Pillow (Anderson and Anderson 227).

Grant asked Buckner, "Where is [Pillow] now?"

Buckner replied, "Gone. He thought you'd rather get hold of him than any other man in the Southern Confederacy."

"Oh," said Grant, "if I had got him, I'd let him go again. He will do us more good commanding you fellows" (Nevin 95).

Grant and Buckner were not the only ones to see the incompetence of Pillow. After Fort Donelson, this time without a sponsor like President Polk, Pillow was reprimanded, suspended, and never given another important command (Boatner 654).

A NECESSARY EVIL

Political generals were a necessity in the Civil War. Allan Millett and Peter Maslowski observe that "even had the failure of many nonprofessionals been predictable, neither Lincoln nor Davis would have dispensed with them. In a people's war requiring mass armies and high morale, using popular leaders made military and political sense. Rallying diverse constituencies, they strengthened national cohesion and determination" (173). These gains, however, were not without costs, and in both the Mexican War and the Civil War, Gideon Pillow proved just how expensive a political general could be.

Stonewall Jackson and the Role of Artillery

During the Mexican War, artillery and infantry were employed in unison consistent with Napoleon's claim that "the better the infantry, the more one must husband and support it with good batteries" (Chandler 179). Thus the United States had organized one company in each artillery regiment as light, or "flying," artillery, designed for use with infantry. These were placed at the point of greatest danger. Accordingly, John Eisenhower writes that "the outcome of a battle, therefore, might well be decided by the performance of a regular lieutenant commanding an artillery company rather than the infantry lieutenant colonel whose regiment he was supporting" (*So Far* 379–380). One lieutenant who filled such a position was Thomas (later Stonewall) Jackson.

In the Mexican War, John Magruder was a captain commanding one of the independent batteries that would follow the flow of the battle. Magruder had a reputation as a fighter, and young Jackson worked hard to join his command. Jackson told a friend, "I wanted to see active service. I wished to be near the enemy and in the fight, and when I heard John Magruder had got his battery, I bent all my energies to be with him, for I knew if there was any fighting to be done, Magruder would be on hand" (Robertson, *Jackson* 60). In Mexico, Jackson would not be disappointed.

But as the Civil War approached, the widespread introduction of the rifle led to artillery losing its Napoleonic advantage. In Mexico, Napoleonic tactics had called for concentrating artillery close up against the enemy's lines to batter a breach through which the infantry could charge. In the Civil War, however, the extended range of rifles allowed the defending infantry, especially when protected by earthworks, to force the artillery to remain so far back that it could not accomplish its Napoleonic effects (Weigley, *American Way* 90). L. van Loan Naisawald explains, "Field artillery could no longer unlimber within easy canister range of the enemy's ranks and at the same time be outside the effective range of the enemy's muskets" (McWhiney and Jamieson 60). Thus, while the Mexican War is replete with examples of artillery in the attack, the most famous uses of artillery in the Civil War are almost exclusively defensive (Beringer et al. 14–15). As a young artilleryman in Mexico, Jackson would experience the devastating offensive power of the artillery at Chapultepec. It was a formula he would struggle to re-create in the Civil War.

CHAPULTEPEC

Chapultepec was a formidable 200-foot-high stronghold that presented the last obstacle barring the way between Winfield Scott and Mexico City. Critical to Scott's plan for this objective was the use of artillery. In fact, Scott had hoped to reduce Chapultepec by artillery fire alone. Thus Scott began his attack on September 12 with a furious fourteen-hour preparatory bombardment. The actual ground assault began the next day.

At 5:30 A.M. on September 13, Scott's batteries initiated a concentrated fire. At 8:00 A.M. the bombardment slackened to allow the infantry to advance. Soon they were caught in a cross fire of Mexican artillery and musket fire. The Americans could neither advance nor retreat.

Jackson had been assigned the role of supporting the Fourteenth Infantry, which was connecting the attacks of Gideon Pillow's and William Worth's divisions. Now Jackson rushed forward with his section of two six-pounders. The enemy fire was intense as Jackson and his men struggled to position the guns. He was able to get one gun across a ditch and into action, but the situation was so tenuous that Worth ordered Jackson to withdraw. Instead, Jackson responded that it was more dangerous to retire than to remain in place. At this time, Magruder arrived on the scene, and he and Jackson, with the help of two or three gunners, manhandled the second gun into position. In the face of this fire, the Mexican artillery was gradually overpowered and the breastwork stormed. It was one of the day's most decisive small unit actions (Robertson, *Jackson* 67; Henderson 40–42).

Pillow stated that "Captain Magruder's field battery, one section of which was served with great gallantry by himself, and the other by his brave Lieut. Jackson, in the face of a galling fire from the enemy's position, did invaluable service preparatory to the general assault" (Robertson, *Jackson* 69). Interestingly, Jackson was one of a very small group that did not despise Pillow. Pillow had ordered Jackson to act independently with his section, and in so doing Jackson wrote he "excited my abiding gratitude." Thereafter Jackson always had respect for Pillow because he had given him "an opportunity to win distinction" (Robertson, *Jackson* 66). It was distinction won through the aggressive offensive use of artillery. Jackson would not forget it.

WHITE OAK SWAMP

Even though Jackson would rise to corps command in the Civil War, his biographers acknowledge his artillery roots. Frank Vandiver observes that Jackson remained an "artillerist always," (161), and James Robertson calls him an "artillerist at heart" (*Jackson* 649).

But Jackson's affection for the artillery reflected his Mexican War experience. Vandiver describes Jackson as "working toward a new use of artillery," one that would answer the question, "Could massed artillery clear the way for the infantry?" (314). This was exactly the Napoleonic use of artillery. Jackson got a chance to test his theory at White Oak Swamp in June 1862.

When Jackson arrived at the swamp, he found that the single bridge crossing had been destroyed. His artillery chief, Colonel Stapleton Crutchfield, had arrived earlier and observed several Federal batteries on line across the swamp. With Jackson's approval, Crutchfield deployed his seven batteries of twenty-three guns for a diagonal line of fire on the Federals (Vandiver 493).

At 1:45 P.M., Jackson's artillery opened fire, catching the Federals by complete surprise. Jackson watched as the Federal batteries limbered up and pulled back. Three shattered guns were left behind. The question now was what would the Federal infantry do. Indeed, some leaped up and ran to the rear, but the main body stood unshaken. As he had brought a lone gun forward at Chapultepec, Jackson now ordered a battery slipped close to the bridge site, directing that it drive off the Federal sharpshooters while Colonel Tom Mun-

Stonewall Jackson. National Archives and Records Administration.

ford's Second Virginia Cavalry rode across the swamp. But Munford's men were quickly repulsed by Federal infantry and artillery.

The Federal artillery had been able to relocate to a new position that was "perfectly sheltered from [the Confederate] guns" (Hill, "Malvern Hill" 387). The situation was exacerbated by the fact that the Federal rifled artillery could outrange the inferior Confederate smoothbore (Dowdey, *Seven Days* 283). This combination of different technology and different terrain than what Jackson had experienced in Mexico had changed the equation. Vandiver writes that the "little excursion had been a lesson in futility" (314–315).

Jackson had a host of problems at White Oak Swamp, not the least of which was his physical and mental exhaustion from the recent Shenandoah Valley Campaign (Krick 66–95). But his experience also illustrates a larger trend in the Civil War. His experiment to replicate the Mexican War formula of concentrated artillery fire to create a breach for the infantry assault had failed. It was a goal that would largely elude his fellow Civil War commanders as well. As such, it is a caution to always consider the impact of technology and terrain on tactics when transferring lessons from one war to another.

James Longstreet
and the Changed Mind?

James Longstreet is one of the more interesting personalities for the student of officers who served in both the Mexican War and the Civil War because information about his personal reflections from Mexico is so scant. In his memoirs, he briefly describes his two major engagements in Mexico but writes nothing about his roles or sentiments about the experience. Instead, he chooses to focus on the exploits of a few of his fellow officers. Late in life, Longstreet returned to Mexico and wrote an unpublished history of the war, but it, too, offers no insight into any personal feelings. Thus any conclusions about lessons Longstreet learned from Mexico are mere speculation, but it appears that Longstreet chose to fight the Civil War differently than he did in Mexico (Wert 38; Piston 6).

OFFENSIVE ACTION IN MEXICO

Longstreet's tactical experience in Mexico was almost entirely spent in small unit offensive operations. Never did he play a purely defensive role in major combat. He led men in battle at Palo Alto, Resaca de la Palma, and Monterey. As an adjutant, he participated, often as a volunteer color-bearer, at San Antonio, Churubusco, El Molino del Rey, and Chapultepec, where he was severely wounded (Piston 6).

Longstreet demonstrated great bravery in Mexico and was often in the thick of serious combat. At Resaca de la Palma, Churubusco, and the attack on Fort Libertad outside Monterey, he fought hand to hand. In the house-to-house fighting at Monterey, Longstreet again experienced a very personal type

BATTLE OF MOLINO DEL REY, FOUGHT SEP! 8!! 1847.
Blowing up the Foundry by the Victorious American Army under Gen! Worth.
Published by James Baillie, 87 th 37 west 2 nd Avenue N.Y.

In Mexico, James Longstreet witnessed the difficulty in attacking strong defenses such as at Molino del Rey. Library of Congress, Prints and Photographs Division, reproduction number LC-USZ62-62219 (b&w film copy neg.)

of combat (Piston 7). At Chapultepec, he was in front of the Eighth Infantry, carrying its colors and leading the way. He was hit with a musket ball in the thigh, fell wounded, and passed the colors to George Pickett. Longstreet's wound was painful and his recovery slow (Wert 45).

From Mexico, Longstreet fully experienced the offensive, but this experience may have "exerted a modifying effect" on his propensity to use it in the future. Churubusco was a close call. In fact, firing from behind formidable earthworks, the Mexicans nearly stopped the Americans cold. It took the courageous example of junior officers like Longstreet to brave the hail of bullets to get the attack moving again. Then at Molino del Rey, Casa Mata provided the Mexicans a strong stone building from which to defend. The Americans were slaughtered and routed. Clearly, Longstreet observed in Mexico that offensive tactics, whether successful or not, could come with a dreadful price (Piston 6–7).

DEFENSIVE LEANINGS IN THE CIVIL WAR

In spite of, or likely because of, Longstreet's offensive experience in Mexico, he adopted a great predilection for the defense in the Civil War. During the Peninsula Campaign, Longstreet fought an excellent rearguard action at Williamsburg that allowed the Confederate artillery and supply train to escape toward Richmond. When participating in offensive operations, however, the results were mixed. Critiquing his overall conduct during the campaign, Longstreet's biographers H. J. Eckenrode and Bryan Conrad summarize that "his offensive tactics at Seven Pines had been wretched. At Gaines's Mill he had handled his men to far better effect, and at Glendale he had conducted a severe offensive action with considerable success. But it still remained true of him that he was essentially a defensive fighter, not offensive, and he was to continue thus to the end of the war" (86).

Longstreet performed well in a defensive role at Fredericksburg. Protected by a stone wall improved with field fortifications, Longstreet's corps "hardly budged an inch under the most intense assault the war had yet seen." William Piston writes, "The implications were not lost on Longstreet" (34). From this experience, Longstreet set out to incorporate a new traverse trench into his fieldworks, with the purpose of withstanding an attack of multiple corps with just one division. Stonewall Jackson was so impressed with what he saw of Longstreet's fortifications along the Rappahannock River that he ordered similar ones prepared in his sector (Piston 34–35; Donovan et al. 201). Indeed, Longstreet always held Fredericksburg in high regard, considering it far superior to the Chancellorsville offensive battle in which he played no part (Longstreet 330).

Longstreet's most famous predilection for the defense involved the Gettysburg Campaign. From the initial planning stages, Longstreet urged Lee to combine the proposed strategic offensive with defensive tactics. Longstreet thought that once the Army of Northern Virginia crossed into Northern territory, the Federals would be compelled to attack. If the Confederates could select a good defensive position from which to receive this attack, they might gain another inexpensive victory, as they did at Fredericksburg (Piston 45). Summing up his views, he writes, "The plan of defensive tactics gave some hope of success, and, in fact, I assured General Lee that the First Corps would receive and defend the battle if he would guard our flanks, leaving the other corps to gather the fruits of success. The First Corps was as solid as a rock— a great rock. It was not to be broken of good position by direct assault, and was steady enough to work and wait for its chosen battle" (Longstreet 334). For Longstreet, the overriding vision, both of the campaign and his corps, is clearly defensive.

Longstreet pursued this line of reasoning after the Confederate victory on the first day of the battle of Gettysburg. He recommended the Confederates move south and east across George Meade's line of communications, find a strong defensive position, and force Meade into a costly attack. Longstreet was surprised when Lee insisted upon attacking instead (Piston 51). Longstreet writes that he told Lee, "We could not call the enemy to position better suited to our plans. All that we have to do is to file around his left and secure good ground between him and his capital." He continues, "This, when said, was thought to be the opinion of my commander as much as my own" (358). Longstreet certainly misread Lee's intentions. In spite of his objections, however, he carried out his orders the next day (Piston 58).

When Lee again pressed the attack on the third day, Longstreet was much more reluctant and seemed to actively search for ways to cancel the assault. Eckenrode and Conrad observe, "Longstreet thus found himself committed to the offensive action he so intensely disliked" (190). Indeed, Longstreet later wrote, "That day at Gettysburg was one of the saddest of my life" (Piston 59–60).

After the war, Longstreet would be part of a bitter debate about Confederate tactics at Gettysburg. William Swinton's history of the war attributed to Longstreet a statement that Lee had promised to remain on the defensive during the campaign. Longstreet never personally made such a claim, but he never denied it either and implied it in his own later writings (Piston 96).

WHY THE CHANGE?

Lee liked to call Longstreet his "Old War Horse," but the moniker certainly cannot carry an offensive connotation. Jeffry Wert concludes, "If Jackson was the army's hammer, Longstreet was its anvil" (206). Longstreet clearly preferred the tactical defense, among other reasons because it spared soldiers' lives (Wert 247).

Perhaps Longstreet had seen too much of the toll exacted by offensive actions in Mexico. Admitting it is speculation, William Piston still wonders, "How did such experiences affect Longstreet in 1861? He probably viewed offensive tactics as highly effective means by which an inferior force might defeat a superior one. But he also knew the cost. Longstreet could never order men into battle without knowing from his own past just what he was asking of the individual soldier" (7). Longstreet's Civil War conduct suggests Piston just may be right.

TECHNOLOGY

Perhaps there is more to Longstreet's predilection for the defense than just his experience in Mexico. Between Mexico and the Civil War, technology had changed, greatly enhancing the strength of the defense at the expense of the offense. Longstreet perhaps intuitively recognized this change when many of his colleagues did not.

It all has to do with the lesson Stonewall Jackson learned about artillery. The increased range of the rifle had given the defense an advantage. When this capability was paired with breastworks, as Longstreet discovered at Fredericksburg, the combination was deadly for the attacker.

The predominant weapon in Mexico was the 1835 model smoothbore flintlock musket. It had a maximum range of about 250 yards but an effective range of maybe 50. Its approximate target-hit ratio at 100 yards was 10 percent. More accurate percussion cap muskets and rifled weapons saw limited use in Mexico, and even at the outbreak of the Civil War the smoothbore musket was the standard weapon (Carney, *Guns* 8). But things were changing. In 1849, after Mexico, Captain Minié in France had made the rifle practical as a mass weapon by developing a bullet with a hollow base that would expand with the gases of the rifle's firing in order to fit the rifling snugly. The United States soon adapted the Model 1855 Springfield rifle to take .58-caliber minié ammunition.

The new technology would require new tactics, and in 1855 the army adopted Major William J. Hardee's *Rifle and Light Infantry Tactics* as its standard. The manual, however, focused on the handling of the new weapon, rather than on its employment. Russell Weigley notes, "The effects upon battlefield tactics were destined to be immense but could not altogether be foreseen and remained to be digested by later tactical writers" (*History* 190).

The change was that the rifle had made the defense stronger. The shortranged smoothbore muskets could get off only one effective shot against an advancing line. The Model 1855 Springfield, with the minié bullet, had an effective range of 200 to 250 yards, allowing a defender to fire many times against an enemy advancing across open ground. The defender's advantage was compounded when he was behind breastworks such as at Fredericksburg. Civil War battles soon demonstrated that rifles could tear a frontal attack to shreds before it could close (Weigley, *History* 235).

Many Civil War generals were slow to recognize the "advances wrought by rifling, the minié ball, and other technological improvements, as well as the morale as discipline of defending troops which made [frontal attacks] problematic at best. The approach cost the lives of many good soldiers" (Carney, *Gateway* 32). Perhaps the bloodshed Longstreet had experienced in Mexico made him more sensitive to this development and led him to realize early that technological changes had made the Civil War a different battlefield.

George Pickett and the Quest for Glory

George Pickett is enshrined in Civil War legend and popular imagination as the leader of the gallant but doomed "Pickett's Charge." His carefully crafted public image, largely the product of the efforts of his wife, casts him as "the epitome of the mythic Southern soldier" (Gordon 2). Interestingly, Pickett had an experience similar in glory to Pickett's Charge as a young lieutenant in Mexico.

GLORY AT CHAPULTEPEC

The last obstacle between Scott and Mexico City was the grouping of buildings, gardens, and groves called Chapultepec. Sitting high atop a hill, Chapultepec was a former Aztec palace and Mexican military college. Walls and gates surrounded the entire complex, and artillery was posted on all sides. An estimated 1,000 Mexican soldiers and cadets defended from inside the enclosure (Gordon 26).

Scott attacked on September 13, 1847, with an artillery bombardment followed by soldiers with ladders and pickaxes assaulting the palace. Scott writes:

At length the ditch and wall of the main work were reached, the scaling ladders brought up and planted by the storming parties; some of the daring spirits first in the assault were cast down—killed

Storming of Chapultepec. Engraving from a painting by W. H. Powell.

or wounded; but a lodgment was soon made; streams of heroes followed; all opposition was overcome, and several of the regimental colors flung out from the upper walls, admist long, continual shouts and cheers, which sent dismay into the capital. No scene could have been more animating or glorious. (Gordon 26)

At the front of the Eighth Infantry, carrying its colors and leading the way, was James Longstreet. Suddenly, Longstreet was hit with a musket ball in the thigh and fell wounded. George Pickett was there to take the colors and continue on. With one hand, Pickett hoisted himself over the ramparts and fought his way to the flagstaff. He tore down the Mexican colors and raised the regiment's. The entire attack took less than an hour. The next day, Mexico City fell (Gordon 27–28).

Pickett's exploits brought him much praise. Scott said Pickett was one of the "most distinguished in those brilliant operations" at Chapultepec. William

Worth cited him as "distinguished for gallantry and zeal." William Montgomery vividly described Pickett's raising of the flag and included him among those "conspicuous for their noble exertions and gallant conduct" (Gordon 28).

Pickett's Mexican War experience "taught him that charging forward with a spirited and determined force could eventually overtake any enemy." It was a war of "frontal charges and flanking attacks that always succeeded, and daring feats that always brought glory. For George Pickett the Mexican War was raising that flag over Chapultepec" (Gordon 28–29). Indeed, Pickett would have a chance to test this theory and relive his glory during the Civil War.

PICKETT'S CHARGE

Pickett would find himself in circumstances similar to Chapultepec on July 3, 1863, at Gettysburg. Now, instead of receiving the flag from his friend Longstreet, he would receive his corps commander Longstreet's order to lead his division in a charge against the Federal center. The comparison to Chapultepec was inescapable, and Pickett's mind drifted back to Mexico as he prepared for the charge. Colonel Birkett Fry reported to discuss coordinations necessary in the plan, and Fry writes that Pickett "appeared to be in excellent spirits, and after a cordial greeting and a pleasant reference to our having been in work of that kind at Chapultepec, expressed great confidence in the ability of our troops to drive the enemy" (Gordon 111). Pickett was full of the optimism—both in himself and his men—that he had learned in Mexico. It was a chance to relive the glory of Chapultepec.

But Gettysburg was not Chapultepec. Instead, it would be a slaughter. With his command staged in the woods on Seminary Ridge, Pickett rode to Longstreet and asked, "General, shall I advance?" Longstreet had been wounded in the same charge that won Pickett fame at Chapultepec. Their different outcomes there perhaps contributed to their different views of tactics in the Civil War. Longstreet had learned the cost of offensive operations. Pickett had learned their glory. Now, the reluctant Longstreet merely nodded, and Pickett was off. His men met a galling fire from the Federal artillery, and gaps soon appeared in the Confederate line. Still the Confederates advanced. Their right and left flanks were broken, with only the center remaining. Ultimately, Lewis Armistead would lead the center to "the high water mark," but, isolated, his men were unable to sustain their attack. Pickett's Charge had failed (Stackpole 260–268).

There was little Pickett could do, and his characteristic optimism turned to despondency. To Longstreet he cried, "General, I am ruined, my division is gone—it is destroyed" (Gordon 116). Even Longstreet, a friend and comrade of twenty years, could not console Pickett.

YET STILL THE GLORY

Pickett's reputation suffered after Gettysburg, as did his performance. Indeed, Lee relieved Pickett from command after his dismal conduct at Five Forks. Yet what Pickett lost at Gettysburg, he was able to recover in the romanticized history of the Confederacy. H. J. Eckenrode and Bryan Conrad explain: "Rarely in the history of the world have men fought with greater bravery and devotion than was [*sic*] shown by the Southerners at Gettysburg, which, in consequence, is an even greater moment to them than to the conquerors. After all, the chief glory of Gettysburg is Pickett's" (213). Indeed, Pickett's Charge is one of the most enduring images of the Lost Cause. William Faulkner in *Intruder in the Dust* perhaps best captures the mystique:

> For every Southern boy, fourteen years old, not once but whenever
> he wants it there is an instant when it's still not yet two o'clock on
> that July afternoon in 1863, the brigades are in position behind the
> rail fence, the guns are laid and ready in the woods and the furled
> flags are already loosened to break out and Pickett himself with his
> long oiled ringlets and his hat in one hand probably and his sword
> in the other looking up the hill waiting for Longstreet to give the
> word and it's all in the balance, it hasn't happened yet, it hasn't even
> begun yet, it not only hasn't begun yet but there is still time for it
> not to begin against that position and those circumstances, which

made more men than Garnett and Kemper and Armistead and Wilcox look grave yet it's going to begin, we all know that, we have come too far with too much at stake and that moment doesn't need even a fourteen-year-old boy to think *This time, Maybe this time* with all this much to lose and all this much to gain. (194–195).

In a way, at Gettysburg, Pickett had his second Chapultepec.

John Pemberton
and Inflexibility

John Pemberton would have two experiences in Mexico that would impact on his later fame as defender of Vicksburg. First, he would serve a significant portion of his time in Mexico as aide to Brigadier General William Jenkins Worth. In Worth, Pemberton would find an example of inflexibility and unsatisfactory people skills that would characterize Pemberton's own personality as a Civil War commander. Second, in Mexico Pemberton would provide a glimpse of his mettle to Lieutenant Ulysses Grant, who would later be Pemberton's antagonist at Vicksburg.

AS WORTH'S AIDE

Pemberton began his service in Mexico serving as an artilleryman under Zachary Taylor. In this capacity, Pemberton was in the midst of thick fighting at Resaca de la Palma. In August 1846, Taylor assigned Pemberton to serve as Worth's aide. Worth had a solid military reputation. He had fought in the War of 1812, served as commandant of cadets at West Point, participated in the Black Hawk War, helped suppress Nat Turner's rebellion, been part of the Cherokee Indian removal from Georgia, and commanded in the Seminole War. But Worth also was vain. Observers described him as "rash and impetuous," "intense and narrow," and "self-centered" (Ballard, *Pemberton* 52). Even his sympathetic biographer Edward Wallace credits Worth with "a petulant contumaciousness" (64). Perhaps the best tactical example of Worth's narrowness is his unsophisticated and costly frontal attack at Molino del Rey. Worth would prove an unfortunate example for Pemberton when it came to broad, responsive, flexible, and anticipatory thought.

Worth's division, and Pemberton with it, was transferred to Scott's army for the campaign against Mexico City. With this change came increased responsibilities to get ready. Pemberton and Worth had already had occasional flare-ups, and the new pressures exacerbated the tension. Pemberton was opinionated and tended to lash back when criticized. After one particularly heated exchange, Pemberton resigned, but Worth smoothed things over, and Pemberton withdrew his resignation. Despite their conflicts, Pemberton gradually grew to like Worth. Pemberton's biographer Michael Ballard concludes that it was an unfortunate pairing. Ballard writes, "Pemberton might have been better served for the future if he had been influenced by a different role model. Worth had an inflexible, sometimes abrupt nature. Colleagues would someday describe Confederate General Pemberton as having the same characteristic." (*Pemberton* 56–57). Indeed, Ballard opines that Pemberton's "own personality would work against his ability to lead men in combat" in the Civil War (*Pemberton* 63).

GRANT'S OBSERVATION

While serving as Worth's aide, Pemberton was observed by fellow lieutenant Ulysses Grant. The two would meet again at Vicksburg. Grant would later remember Pemberton's conduct in Mexico, writing, "A more conscientious, honorable man never lived. I remember when a general order was issued that none of the junior officers should be allowed horses during marches. Mexico is not an easy country to march in. Young officers not accustomed to it soon got footsore. This was quickly discovered, and they were found lagging behind. But the order was not revoked, yet a verbal permit was accepted, and nearly all of them remounted. Pemberton alone said, No, he would walk, as the order was still extant not to ride, and he did walk, though suffering intensely the while." Grant claimed that his recollection of this incident would convince him at Vicksburg that Pemberton would not easily yield. Grant concludes the story saying, "This

I thought of all the time [Pemberton] was in Vicksburg and I outside of it; and I knew he would hold on to the last" (Pemberton 14).

PEMBERTON AT VICKSBURG

On October 1, 1862, Major General Pemberton was appointed commander of the Confederate forces in Mississippi and that part of Louisiana east of the Mississippi River. He approached these duties in bureaucratic fashion, providing sound organizing and systematizing functions, but little contribution to battlefield leadership and military science (Ballard, *Pemberton* 116). Ballard observes that Pemberton "operated as though he were still an aide to General Worth, directing, deploying, and watching over operations. . . . [H]e indicated that he viewed his job as that of an administrator, not a combat general" (*Pemberton* 129). As Grant began presenting Pemberton with multiple threats and diversions, Pemberton became confused and paralyzed. One diversion was a cavalry raid led by Benjamin Grierson out of Tennessee into Mississippi. Pemberton, "[w]ho was much better at dealing with the known than with the suspected," focused on Grierson while Grant, the real threat, was sneaking in the back door (Ballard, *Vicksburg* 24).

As Grant closed in, Pemberton was left with a choice—defend from Vicksburg or strike Grant. His commander, Joe Johnston, ordered him to unite his forces and attack Grant, even if that meant abandoning Vicksburg. Conversely, President Jefferson Davis instructed Pemberton to "hold both Vicksburg and Port Hudson" (Arnold 125). Pemberton lacked the flexibility to deal with such a confused and complicated situation.

By April 30, the Federal navy had successfully passed the Confederate positions both at Vicksburg and Grand Gulf, and Grant's army had crossed the Mississippi River unopposed at Bruinsburg. Pemberton seems to have understood intellectually the significance of these developments, writing President Davis on May 1 that the "enemy's success in passing our batteries has completely changed the character of defense." However, James Arnold succinctly concludes, "Whether Pemberton had the mental flexibility to adjust to the new situation was the pressing question. He needed to ask himself what was

Pemberton, Lieut.-Gen. J. C., of................Va.

7068 d

John Pemberton. Library of Congress, Prints and Photographs Division, reproduction number LC-USZ62-130838 (b&w film copy neg.).

Vicksburg's value if it could not interdict the river. After Grant crossed the river, [Pemberton] needed to change his focus from holding the city to defeating Grant's army" (117). Pemberton would not adjust.

Instead, Pemberton chose to defend Vicksburg. In so doing, he surrendered the initiative and the advantages of maneuver and the offensive to Grant. By July 4, Pemberton would surrender.

A successful defense requires flexibility. Commanders must focus their planning on preparations in depth, use of reserves, and the ability to shift the main effort (FM 3-0, 8-3). Pemberton failed to display this flexibility. He did not anticipate Grant crossing the Mississippi south of Vicksburg. In fact, he believed Grant had abandoned the effort and withdrawn toward Memphis. He inefficiently diverted units from his strategic reserve to chase after Grierson's diversion. Finally, he failed to shift his main effort from defending Vicksburg to defeating Grant when the situation required (Arnold 74, 87, 117). Moreover, strategic leaders must demonstrate the flexibility to handle competing demands, even in an uncertain and ambiguous environment (FM 22-100 7-9). Such prerequisites lay beyond Pemberton's capabilities. Ballard notes at Vicksburg "[m]uch was going on, and Pemberton had lost control of it . . . he had been reduced to a state of total uncertainty" (*Pemberton* 140). Arnold agrees, writing, "War's uncertainty continued to vex Pemberton. . . . In the absence of certain intelligence and for fear of making a misstep, Pemberton remained passive" (121).

Assuredly, there are many contributing factors to Pemberton's poor leadership at Vicksburg. He is a classic example of the Peter Principle, having been promoted beyond the limits of his abilities. His earlier Civil War experience at Charleston, South Carolina, had taught him to focus on terrain rather than on the enemy. He had a troublesome relationship with some of his key subordinates. All of these factors helped paralyze Pemberton when he was confronted with a dynamic and changing situation at Vicksburg. To make matters worse was the compounding problem that in his formative years in Mexico under Worth's tutelage, Pemberton had not developed the flexibility he would need at Vicksburg.

A. P. Hill and the
Tendency to Criticize

Fellow Confederate brigadier general James Walker asserted that "of all the Confederate leaders [Ambrose Powell Hill] was the most genial and lovable in his disposition" (Robertson, *Hill* 326). Walker notwithstanding, Hill's biographer William Hassler notes, "However, beneath Hill's genial exterior smoldered a nervous and sensitive nature. He was extremely volatile and quick to take offense, especially if an act violated his punctilious concept of justice or protocol" (4). Often this characteristic would manifest itself in criticism of others, and Hill had no fear of differing with his superiors (Waugh 379). Hill's quick pen and tongue would cause General Robert E. Lee tiresome grief in the Army of Northern Virginia. A study of Hill's brief service in Mexico reveals that Lee should not have been surprised.

OBSERVATIONS IN MEXICO

Graduating from West Point in 1847, Hill caught only the tail end of the Mexico War, and his service was limited, amounting to what Hassler terms "disappointingly minor fighting" (15). As acting adjutant, Hill guarded the wagon trains as his battalion fought at Huamantla. He saw some action at Puebla and the mopping-up operations that followed, but he also spent a fair amount of time battling typhoid fever. Nonetheless, Hill thought he had seen and done enough to be sharply critical of some of his superiors. To Hill, Brigadier General William Worth was "a weak headed, vain glorious, but brave man, perfectly reckless of the lives of his soldiers and his own." Major General

Gideon Pillow was "as soft as his name and will no doubt be dismissed from the Army for barefaced lying." Major General William Butler was "a general of mushroom growth, over whom I, young as I am, can claim some three years military experience" (Robertson, *Hill* 15–18). This early glimpse of Hill's sharp and caustic tongue and his willingness to direct it at his superiors would reappear in the Civil War in his dealings with James Longstreet and Stonewall Jackson.

THE TREND CONTINUES

After Mexico, Hill served a variety of assignments, including almost five years in the Office of the Superintendent of the U.S. Coast Survey. Douglas Southall Freeman notes that this posting gave Hill "a certain knowledge of the inner workings of the machinery of government but it had not improved his temper" (*Lee's Lieutenants* 1:xlix). Nonetheless, Hill was a fighter. He was promoted to brigadier general on February 26, 1862, and given a brigade, which he led at Williamsburg. Promotion to major general followed on May 26, and Hill "emerged from the Peninsular Campaign with the reputation of being one of the best combat officers Lee had" (Robertson, *Hill* 95).

Hill's legitimate accomplishments, however, were inflated by the newspaper reports of John Daniel. Furthermore, Daniel's exaggerations came at the expense of James Longstreet, and Longstreet voiced his chagrin. Now it was Hill's turn to get angry. He fired off a terse message to General Lee, which Longstreet endorsed, in which Hill requested to be relieved from Longstreet's command. Next Hill refused communications from Major Moxley Sorrel, Longstreet's assistant adjutant general. On Longstreet's order, Sorrel placed Hill under arrest. An exchange of heated letters ensued, and Hill ultimately challenged Longstreet to a duel. Lee was forced to intervene, and thereafter relations between Hill and Longstreet were "at best coldly courteous" (Robertson, *Hill* 97).

Hill was too good a commander to keep under arrest, and he clearly was needed in the field. Hoping to remove the tensions between Hill and Longstreet, Lee placed Hill under Stonewall Jackson's command. The decision marked the beginning of "one of the Civil War's most heated and damaging

A. P. Hill. National Archives and Records
Administration.

feuds" (Robertson, *Hill* 98). Hill already believed Jackson had performed poorly at Mechanicsville, and now Jackson's characteristic reticence further irritated Hill. The tension reached the crisis point on August 8, 1862, when Jackson's secrecy left Hill befuddled about the order of a march from Orange to Culpepper, Virginia. Jackson's garbled, incomplete, and seemingly arbitrary orders continued throughout the battle of Cedar Mountain, on the next march to Gordonsville, and in bivouac at White Sulphur Springs (Robertson, *Hill* 102–110).

The worst, however, was yet to come. The relations between Hill and Jackson at Second Manassas would be so low that Robertson titles that chapter of his biography of Hill "Fighting Pope—and Jackson" (Robertson, *Hill* 117). Again, the crisis point was reached while on the march. Jackson was upset to find Hill's men not marching at the hour Jackson had appointed. Jackson intervened in a manner that Hill took to be usurping his command and, presenting Jackson the hilt of his sword, told Jackson, "If you take command of my troops in my presence, take my sword also" (Robertson, *Hill* 131). Jackson placed Hill under arrest, Hill's second arrest in two months. Robertson notes that by now, "[b]etween Hill and Jackson was a personal breach that would never heal" (*Hill* 132).

This quarrel between two of his key lieutenants was the last thing Lee needed as he prepared for the Antietam campaign. Even Jackson realized the necessity of the situation, and, at Hill's request, Jackson restored Hill to command for the present campaign, after which he would return to arrest (Robertson, *Hill* 134–135). Hill preformed well at Harper's Ferry and even better at Antietam, where Robertson terms him "the hero of the hour" (Robertson, *Hill* 147).

Upon the army's return to Virginia, however, matters picked up where they left off. Hill forwarded a letter to Lee that stated, "I respectfully represent that I deem myself to have been treated with injustice and censured and punished at the head of my command and request that a Court of Inquiry be granted me." Jackson endorsed the request, adding a note that "I found that under [Hill's] successor, General Branch, my orders were much better carried out." This was quite a dilemma for Lee. Jackson's authority had to be respected, but Lee could not afford to lose Hill, one of Lee's best generals, either. Lee had to decide a battle of wills between Hill the firebrand and Jackson the glacier (Robertson, *Hill* 152–153).

Lee tried to sidestep the issue, returning Hill's request with the annotation that Hill's "attention being now called to what appeared to be a neglect of duty by his commander, but which from an officer of his character could not be intentional and I feel assured will never be repeated, I see no advantage to the service in further investigating this matter nor could it without detriment be done at this time." Hill would have none of this. To him, it was an admission of guilt, and on September 30 he again asked for a court of inquiry. This time he added a reference to Jackson as "the officer who abuses his authority to punish, and then sustains his punishment by making loose charges against an officer who had done and is doing his utmost to make his troops efficient" (Robertson, *Hill* 153).

Lee tried to mediate the situation, bringing Hill and Jackson together for several hours, but neither officer would budge. After that, Hill and Jackson communicated as briefly and as formally as possible. Lee could only hope that the passing of time would resolve the argument. He shelved the paperwork and got on with his more important tasks of commanding general (Robertson, *Hill* 154).

Jackson seemed content to let the matter die, but for Hill it was still a burning issue. In a November letter to Jeb Stuart, Hill criticized Jackson as "that crazy old Presbyterian fool" and opined, "The Almighty will get tired, helping Jackson after awhile, and then he'll get the damndest thrashing—and the shoe pinches, for I should get my share and probably all the blame, for the people will never blame Stonewall for any disaster" (Robertson, *Hill* 157).

The running feud with Jackson doubtless affected Hill's lackluster performance at Fredericksburg (Robertson, *Hill* 168), and in the lull in military operations that followed, Hill renewed his war of words. Again he pressed Lee for a trial. Lee was in quite a spot. Two of his three highest-ranking generals were barely speaking to each other, and there were no signs that the argument was going to subside.

Lee sent Hill a carefully worded letter, outlining his position: "I do not think that in every case where an officer is arrested there is necessity for a trial by court-martial and I consider yours one in which such a proceeding is unnecessary" (Robertson, *Hill* 171). Lee returned an endorsement to Jackson to the effect that there be no trial.

Still, Hill would not acquiesce. Near the end of January he again wrote Lee, demanding a trial and informing Lee that he had been forced "to preserve every scrap of paper received from Corps Hd. Qrs. to guard myself against any new eruption from this slumbering volcano" (Robertson, *Hill* 172).

Lee, obviously frustrated, did not reply, and the matter simmered under the surface for two more months, only to be renewed after Cedar Mountain. Hill's report was naturally slanted in his favor, and his accounts of "slow marches" infuriated Jackson. Jackson launched a detailed investigation and then added an endorsement to Hill's report, which was basically a point-by-point rebuttal. Hill responded with a period of extreme pettiness whenever Jackson exercised authority. Finally, things escalated to the point that on April 24, 1863, Jackson sent Lee a lengthy set of documents relating to Hill accompanied by a letter stating, "I respectfully request that Genl. Hill be relieved from duty in my Corps" (Robertson, *Hill* 172–175).

Ultimately, the only thing that would end the feud was the mortal wounding of Jackson at Chancellorsville on May 2. Hill was with Jackson at the time, and momentarily setting his anger aside, he ministered to Jackson's wounds and tried to comfort him. Hill told Jackson, "I will try to keep your accident from the knowledge of the troops."

"Thank you," replied Jackson (Robertson, *Hill* 188–189).

It was the last conversation the two would have before Jackson died. Finally, the Hill-Jackson war of words was over. On April 2, 1865, in the waning days of the Confederacy, Hill, too, would be killed in action.

THE ELUSIVE PERSONALITY OF A. P. HILL

Two of the generals who felt the sting of Hill's criticism in Mexico, William Worth and Gideon Pillow, would end the Mexican War embroiled in controversial courts of inquiry such as Hill sought as his vindication in the Civil War. Hill was a hard fighter and a man upon whom Lee increasingly depended, yet he had what Douglas Southall Freeman called an "elusive personality" (Hassler xiii). Part of this characteristic was a quick and critical tongue, which would first show itself in Mexico and then reappear as an unfortunate distraction to Robert E. Lee in the Civil War.

LEWIS ARMISTEAD
AND COMRADES
BECOMING ENEMIES

The shared hardships of war are a fertile ground for the formation of life-long friendships. Lewis Armistead and Winfield Scott Hancock shared such hardships during their service together as lieutenants in Mexico. Robert Selph Henry writes that at Chapultepec,

> [m]en of all commands, intermingled, leaped into the ditch and fought to get the ladders up, so they could mount them. First into the ditch was Lieutenant Lewis A. Armistead, of the Sixth Infantry. Almost immediately he was wounded. He was to be wounded again on the field of battle sixteen years later as, with hat on the point of his sword, he waved to his brigade to follow him over the stone wall of the cemetery at Gettysburg—and to die that night in the hospital of the corps commanded by Major General Winfield Scott Hancock, his fellow lieutenant in the Sixth at the storming of Chapultepec. (*Mexican War* 361)

The story of these two friends has come to epitomize the tragedy of comrades in Mexico becoming enemies in the Civil War.

CHAPULTEPEC, THE AZTEC CLUB, AND BEYOND

As the Sixth Infantry pressed on to Mexico City, Hancock fought side by side with a number of other officers who would win fame in the Civil War—Lewis

Armistead, Simon Buckner, James Longstreet, and John Sedgwick among them. Hancock took command when his company commander was wounded at Churubusco and was subsequently brevetted to first lieutenant. Hancock was again in front at Molino del Rey. Next came Chapultepec, but here romanticism and history diverge. The frequently recorded account of how Longstreet, Pickett, Armistead, and Hancock—men who would all meet again at Gettysburg—stormed the citadel side by side is mere legend. In fact, Hancock had succumbed to chills and fever after Molino del Rey and was sick in his tent at the prelude to the final assault. Nonetheless, when the fighting began, he wrapped himself in a blanket and crawled to the roof of the nearest house to gain a view of the battle. "The balls whizzed around me," he wrote, "but I kept my post, doing what I could; and when I learned that the colors I saw hoisted on the conquered walls were those of my own regiment, my heart beat quick at the glorious sight" (Tucker, *Hancock* 42).

Hancock recovered sufficiently to join in the final four days of fighting and the capture of Mexico City. With the occupation of Mexico, certain signs of normality entered the soldiers' lives. One was the opening of an officers' club, the Aztec Club, on October 13, 1847. Among its members were "most of the major figures in the Mexican War army and a large group whose fame would come a decade and a half later" (Bauer 327). Hancock was an original member. Armistead would join later.

After Mexico, Hancock and many of his Mexican War comrades would find themselves serving at various posts in the western United States. The inescapable approach of the Civil War would force the old friends to choose sides. Many Southerners gathered in Los Angeles, seeking transportation back to their native states. Hancock was serving there as a quartermaster. On June 15, 1861, Hancock hosted a farewell party for his friends, many from the Sixth Infantry, as they departed for their separate sides in the Civil War.

Among those present was Lewis Armistead, whom Hancock's biographer Glenn Tucker describes as "the most deeply affected" of those gathered. Tucker writes that Armistead

> seemed to sense the bitter finality of parting with Hancock, alongside whom he had fought at Churubusco, served in the Everglades and made the long, toiling march across the plains and mountains from Fort Leavenworth to Benicia [California]. His tears, streaming

down his face, were contagious. He put his hands on Hancock's shoulders, looked him in the eye and said: "Hancock, good-by. You can never know what this has cost me, and I hope God will strike me dead if I am ever induced to leave my native soil, should worst come to worst." (*Hancock* 65)

Then Armistead entrusted Hancock's wife, Almira, with a small satchel of personal items and mementos to be opened only in the event Armistead was killed.

Almira Hancock did not give a full list of those at the farewell party, but she did say that three of the six who left that midnight were killed in front of her husband's lines at Gettysburg. Indeed, after Gettysburg she would have cause to open Armistead's satchel (Tucker, *Hancock* 64–65).

GETTYSBURG

The most poignant account of Armistead's friendship with Hancock is romanticized in Michael Shaara's novel *Killer Angels*. As Shaara imagines it, at the end of the second day at Gettysburg, Longstreet and Armistead are recalling the day's events. Armistead tells Longstreet, Hancock is "the best they've got, and that's a fact."

"Yep," agrees Longstreet.

"Like to go on over and see him, soon's I can, if it's all right," says Armistead.

"Sure. Maybe tomorrow," replies Longstreet (Shaara 262).

Indeed, Armistead will go over to Hancock "tomorrow," but it will be for an attack rather than a friendly visit. In Shaara's version, as Lee tells Longstreet of his planned attack, Longstreet looks at Cemetery Ridge and muses, "Hancock is up there."

Lee nods, "Yes, that's the Second Corps."

"Hard on Armistead," Longstreet sighs (Shaara 320).

Shaara describes how Armistead recalls his last evening with Hancock in California as he prepares for the attack, then just before he begins, Armistead says to himself, "Win, I'm sorry" (Shaara 326). And so Pickett's Charge began.

As the left and right flanks of the attackers withered away, only the center re-mained as a forlorn hope. Their objective was a low stone wall on the western slope of Cemetery Ridge. Defending there was Winfield Scott Hancock and his Second Corps. Leading the attack was Lewis Armistead and his brigade of five Virginia regiments.

One hundred and fifty Confederates poured over the wall and momen-tarily broke the Federal line. However, the defenders recovered, rushed for-ward fresh artillery, and opened fire less than ten yards from Armistead and his men. Federals closed in from all sides. Armistead reached a captured Fed-eral cannon, put his hand on it, and was shot. It was "the high water mark" of the Confederacy (Stackpole 267).

As Armistead lay dying, Hancock rode to another part of the battlefield. While conferring with Brigadier General George Stannard, Hancock was struck in the right thigh by a minié ball that had passed through the pommel of his saddle. As the bullet continued into Hancock's groin, it carried with it bits of wood and a nail from the saddle (Tucker, *Hancock* 156–157). In spite of the excruciatingly painful wound, Hancock remained on the field until he was certain victory was assured.

Hancock spent the fall and winter recovering, rejoining the army on March 23, 1864. Armistead was not so fortunate. He was taken prisoner, and, as the life slipped away from him, he asked that his captors deliver a message to his old friend Hancock. Accounts vary, but Armistead reportedly said words to the effect of "Tell General Hancock for me that I have done him and done you all an injury which I shall regret the longest day I live." The exact mean-ing of Armistead's words has been much debated, but at least one conclusion is that Armistead had learned of Hancock's wound and was filled with grief by the part he had played in harming his old friend (Tucker, *Hancock* 160–164). Such a rendering is certainly the epitome of a war that found so many com-rades from Mexico on opposite sides.

Summary of
Lessons Learned

What are the general conclusions that can be drawn from this effort to understand the Civil War in light of a man's experience in Mexico? It is a difficult question because many Mexican War veterans seem to have left the war with different lessons. Robert E. Lee learned to use reconnaissance to find a way to conduct a turning movement, while P. G. T. Beauregard viewed the turning movement with askance and remained true to the frontal attack. Ulysses Grant learned to take logistical risk, while George Thomas learned to be logistically cautious. Confederate Jefferson Davis learned to place too much confidence in his own abilities, while William Sherman learned to recognize his limitations. James Longstreet learned the fearful casualties of the offensive, while George Pickett learned to love its glory. George McClellan learned to be cautious and deliberate, while Phil Kearny learned to be bold and recklessly daring.

Other lessons are more consistent. Both John Slidell and Samuel Du Pont learned to view war on an international level. Joe Hooker, Henry Halleck, and John Winder learned administrative lessons, though Winder found not all were transferable. John Pemberton, Federal Jefferson Davis, and A. P. Hill exhibited personality traits that would remain consistent in the Civil War. Henry Hunt and Stonewall Jackson would both struggle with adapting artillery tactics to the technologically changed battlefield. Braxton Bragg and Lewis Armistead would both build personal relationships in Mexico that would follow them into the Civil War.

How, then, can one explain the varied lessons? At least three factors seem to be of importance—the commander under whom the individual served, the individual's personal experience with success or failure, and the individual's ability to apply what he learned in one situation to another.

The most telling impact of leadership on the junior officer corps in Mexico was determined by whom the officer served under. Those who served under Winfield Scott witnessed the era's most professional soldier in action. They learned the importance of reconnaissance, how to avoid casualties by turning the enemy, and how a commander uses his staff. However, they also learned a way of waging war in a limited fashion that would lose much of its relevance by the time of the Civil War. While Scott's leadership and tactics survived the Mexican War, his overall approach to warfare did not.

Junior officers who served under Zachary Taylor learned a much more informal leadership style, which was effective at the local unit level because of its strong personal example but was of much less value in the broader perspective. They learned little of staff operations or sophisticated strategy. Soldiers under Taylor may have learned how to fight, but they did not learn how to wage war.

Thus by serving under Scott, Lee learned to value reconnaissance; Grant learned to take calculated risks; McClellan learned to wage limited war. By serving under Taylor, Davis learned to be self-reliant; Pope learned a callous attitude toward civilians; Meade learned to play it safe. Commanders at lower levels also influenced their subordinates. Pemberton learned inflexibility serving under William Worth. McClellan learned to distrust politicians serving under Gideon Pillow. Hooker was forced to learn administrative skills serving as chief of staff for a host of marginal commanders who did not have many. Hunt learned how to employ artillery under James Duncan. The individual's commander made a big difference in what the individual experienced and perhaps learned.

Second, it is natural to repeat tactics that achieved positive results and avoid those that did not. Individuals who saw something work in Mexico tried it again in the Civil War. Grant saw Scott successfully reduce his line of supply on the march to Mexico, and Grant repeated the tactic in the Vicksburg Campaign. Lee saw Scott successfully execute turning movements at places like Cerro Gordo, and Lee repeated the maneuver at Chancellorsville and elsewhere. Pickett found glory in the frontal assault at Chapultepec and was eager to repeat it at Gettysburg.

Other individuals had negative experiences in Mexico that caused them to try something different in the Civil War. Thomas experienced a close brush with logistical disaster at Fort Brown and resolved not to put himself in the same situation at Nashville. Longstreet saw the carnage of frontal attacks and was himself wounded at Chapultepec. In the Civil War, he would thus favor the defense. Samuel Du Pont would see how a blockade suffered from insufficient resupply points in Mexico and would ensure the Civil War blockade was supported by adequate bases. Naturally, Mexican War veterans sought to emulate success and avoid failure.

However, a successful tactic in the Mexican War would not always survive the changes in technology or other unique situations in the Civil War. The measure of a great Civil War general was his ability to apply what he had learned in Mexico, not blindly repeat or avoid it. Many had trouble with this.

At the strategic level, Scott failed to appreciate the changing nature of warfare and proposed a limited strategy that worked in Mexico but was politically inappropriate for the Civil War. Operationally, McClellan saw the siege effectively used at Vera Cruz but tried to repeat it at Yorktown when the situation required offensive maneuver. Tactically, Jackson sought to continue to use artillery in the close-in offensive role when Civil War technology had made such employment routinely impractical. Administratively, Winder tried to use the same heavy-handed governance techniques against his fellow Southerners that had been better suited for the conquered Mexicans. Mexico may have been a rehearsal for the Civil War, but the lessons of history must always be put in context.

Mexico, then, was to have a profound effect on the leadership of the Civil War. Many of the generals, admirals, and politicians of the Civil War were shaped by their experience in the Mexican War, for better or for worse. For the good ones, Mexico was indeed "an arch to build upon"—not an end unto itself but a solid foundation to carry them from one experience to the next.

Appendix A lists 194 Federal generals who served in the Mexican War. Appendix B lists 142 Confederates who did the same. It is hard to imagine a more profound legacy from one war to the next.

Appendix A.

FEDERAL CIVIL WAR GENERALS WHO ALSO SERVED IN THE MEXICAN WAR

Abercrombie, John Joseph
Allen, Robert
Alvord, Benjamin
Anderson, Robert
Arnold, Lewis Golding
Augur, Christopher Columbus
Baker, Edward Dickinson
Barnard, John Gross
Barnes, Joseph K
Barry, William Farquhar
Beatty, Samuel
Benham, Henry Washington
Benton, William Plummer
Bohlen, Henry
Brannan, John Milton
Brooks, William Thomas Harbaugh
Buchanan, Robert Christie
Buell, Don Carlos
Burnside, Ambrose Everett
Cadwalader, George
Campbell, Charles Thomas
Campbell, William Bowen
Canby, Edward Richard Sprigg
Carleton, James Henry
Casey, Silas
Clay, Cassius Marcellus
Connor, Patrick Edward

Cooke, Philip St George
Cooper, Joseph Alexander
Couch, Darius Nash
Craig, James
Crittenden, Thomas Leonidas
Crittenden, Thomas Turpin
Curtis, Samuel Ryan
Dana, Napoleon Jackson Tecumseh
Davidson, John Wynn
Davis, Jefferson Columbus
Dent, Frederick Tracy
Denver, James William
De Russy, Gustavus Adolphus
Doubleday, Abner
Dumont, Ebenezer
Dyer, Alexander Brydie
Eaton, Amos Beebe
Elliot, Washington Lafayette
Emory, William Hemsley
Foster, John Gray
Franklin, William Buel
French, William Henry
Fry, James Barnet
Fry, Speed Smith
Garrard, Theophilus Toulmin
Geary, John White
Getty, George Washington

Gibbon, John
Gibbs, Alfred
Gilbert, Charles Champion
Gordon, George Henry
Gorman, Willis Arnold
Graham, Charles Kinnaird
Graham, Lawrence Pike
Granger, Gordon
Grant, Ulysses Simpson
Griffin, Charles
Halleck, Henry Wager
Hamilton, Charles Smith
Hamilton, Schuyler
Hancock, Winfield Scott
Harney, William Selby
Haskin, Joseph Abel
Hatch, John Porter
Haynie, Isham Nicholas
Hays, Alexander
Hays, William
Heckman, Charles Adam
Heintzelman, Samuel Peter
Hobson, Edward Henry
Hooker, Joseph
Howe, Albion Parris
Hunt, Lewis Cass
Ingalls, Rufus
Jackson, Conrad Feger
Jackson, James Streshly
Judah, Henry Moses
Kautz, August Valentine
Kearny, Philip
Kenly, John Reese
Kimball, Nathan
King, John Haskell
Knipe, Joseph Farmer
Lawler, Michael Kelly
Logan, John Alexander
Lucas, Thomas John
Lyon, Nathaniel
Lytle, William Haynes

Maltby, Jasper Adalmorn
Mansfield, Joseph King Fenno
Manson, Mahlon Dickerson
Marcy, Randolph Barnes
McCall, George Archibald
McClellan, George Brinton
McDowell, Irvin
McGinnis, George Francis
McKean, Thomas Jefferson
McKinstry, Justus
McMillan, James Winning
Meade, George Gordon
Milroy, Robert Huston
Mitchell, Robert Byington
Montgomery, William Reading
Morell, George Webb
Morgan, George Washington
Morgan, James Dada
Mott, Gershom
Mower, Joseph Anthony
Nagle, James
Naglee, Henry Morris
Negley, James Scott
Nelson, William
Oglesby, Richard James
Ord, Edward Otho Cresap
Palmer, Innis Newton
Patterson, Francis Engle
Paul, Gabriel René
Peck, John James
Phelps, John Wolcott
Pitcher, Thomas Gamble
Pleasonton, Alfred
Pope, John
Porter, Andrew
Porter, Fitz John
Potter, Joseph Haydn
Prentiss, Benjamin Mayberry
Prince, Henry
Ramsay, George Douglas
Reno, Jesse Lee

Revere, Joseph Warren
Reynolds, John Fulton
Richardson, Israel Bush
Ricketts, James Brewerton
Ripley, James Wolfe
Roberts, Benjamin Stone
Robinson, John Cleveland
Ross, Leonard Fulton
Rousseau, Lovell Harrison
Rowley, Thomas Algeo
Rucker, Daniel Henry
Russell, David Allen
Scammon, Eliakim Parker
Sedgwick, John
Seymour, Truman
Shackelford, James Murrell
Sherman, Thomas West
Sherman, William Tecumseh
Shields, James
Smith, Charles Ferguson
Smith, Green Clay
Steele, Frederick
Stevens, Isaac Ingalls
Stone, Charles Pomeroy
Stoneman, George
Sturgis, Samuel Davis
Sully, Alfred
Sumner, Edwin Vose
Sweeny, Thomas William
Sykes, George
Taylor, George William
Taylor, Joseph Pannell
Taylor, Nelson
Thomas, George Henry
Thomas, Lorenzo
Todd, John Blair Smith
Totten, Joseph Gilbert
Tower, Zealous Bates
Van Derveer, Ferdinand
Van Vliet, Stewart
Viele, Egbert Ludovicus

Von Steinwehr, Baron Adolph Wilhelm
    August Friedrich
Wallace, Lewis
Wallace, William H. Lamb
Ward, John Henry Hobart
Ward, William Thomas
Webster, Joseph Dana
Welsh, Thomas
Wessells, Henry Walton
West, Joseph Rodman
Whitaker, Walter Chiles
Willcox, Orlando Bolivar
Williams, Alpheus Starkey
Williams, Seth
Williams, Thomas
Wood, Thomas John
Wool, John Ellis
Wright, George

Appendix B.

CONFEDERATE CIVIL WAR GENERALS WHO
ALSO SERVED IN THE MEXICAN WAR

Adams, John
Anderson, George Thomas
Anderson, James Patton
Anderson, Richard Heron
Anderson, Samuel Read
Archer, James Jay
Armistead, Lewis Addison
Barksdale, William
Bate, William Brimage
Beauregard, Pierre Gustave Toutant
Bee, Barnard Elliott
Bee, Hamilton Prioleau
Blanchard, Albert Gallatin
Bonham, Milledge Luke
Bragg, Braxton
Bryan, Goode
Buckner, Simon Bolivar
Buford, Abraham
Cantey, James
Cheatham, Benjamin Franklin
Chilton, Robert Hall
Churchill, Thomas James
Clanton, James Holt
Clark, Charles
Colquitt, Alfred Holt
Cooper, Douglas Hancock
Corse, Montgomery Dent

Crittenden, George Bibb
Davidson, Henry Brevard
Deas, Zachariah Cantey
Dunovant, John
Early, Jubal Anderson
Elzey (Jones), Arnold
Ewell, Richard Stoddert
Fagan, James Fleming
Forney, William Henry
French, Samuel Gibbs
Frost, Daniel Marsh
Fry, Birkett Davenport
Gardner, Franklin
Gardner, William Montgomery
Garnett, Robert Seldon
Gatlin, Richard Caswell
Gladden, Adley Hogan
Grayson, John Breckinridge
Green, Thomas
Greer, Elkanah Brackin
Gregg, Maxcy
Griffith, Richard
Hanson, Roger Weightman
Hardee, William Joseph
Hardeman, William Polk
Harrison, Thomas
Hawes, James Morrison

Hays, Harry Thompson
Hébert, Paul Octave
Hill, Ambrose Powell
Hill, Daniel Harvey
Hindman, Thomas Carmichael
Hogg, Joseph Lewis
Holmes, Theophilus Hunter
Huger, Benjamin
Iverson, Alfred Jr
Jackson, Henry Rootes
Jackson, Thomas Jonathan
Johnson, Bushrod Rust
Johnson, Edward
Johnston, Albert Sidney
Johnston, Joseph Eggleston
Jones, David Rumph
Jordan, Thomas
Kemper, James Lawson
Kershaw, Joseph Brevard
Lane, Walter Paye
Lee, Robert Edward
Little, Lewis Henry
Longstreet, James
Loring, William Wing
Lovell, Mansfield
Lowrey, Mark Perrin
Mackall, William Whann
Magruder, John Bankhead
Maney, George Earl
Manigault, Arthur Middleton
Marshall, Humphrey
Martin, James Green
Maury, Dabney Herndon
Maxey, Samuel Bell
McCown, John Porter
McCulloch, Henry Eustace
McGowan, Samuel
McLaws, Lafayette
McNair, Evander
Miller, William
Morgan, John Hunt

Nelson, Allison
Parsons, Mosby Monroe
Pemberton, John Clifford
Perrin, Abner Monroe
Pettus, Edmund Winston
Pickett, George Edward
Pike, Albert
Pillow, Gideon Johnson
Posey, Carnot
Preston, William
Price, Sterling
Rains, Gabriel James
Ripley, Roswell Sabine
Roane, John Seldon
Ruggles, Daniel
Scurry, William Read
Sibley, Henry Hopkins
Slack, William Yarnel
Slaughter, James Edwin
Smith, Edmund Kirby
Smith, Gustavus Woodson
Smith, Martin Luther
Smith, William Duncan
Stafford, Leroy Augustus
Steele, William
Stevenson, Carter Littlepage
Taliaferro, William Booth
Taylor, Richard
Taylor, Thomas Hart
Thomas, Edward Lloyd
Tilghman, Lloyd
Trapier, James Heyward
Twiggs, David Emanuel
Van Dorn, Earl
Vaughn, John Crawford
Walker, John George
Walker, William Henry Talbot
Walker, William Stephen
Waterhouse, Richard
Wayne, Henry Constantine
Weisiger, David Addison

Whitfield, John Wilkins
Wilcox, Cadmus Marcellus
Williams, John Stuart
Winder, John Henry
Withers, Jones Mitchell
Wofford, William Tatum

WORKS CITED

Amero, Richard. "The Mexican-American War in Baja California." *Journal of San Diego History* 30:1 (1984): 49–64.

Anderson, Nancy Scott, and Dwight Anderson. *The Generals: Ulysses S. Grant and Robert E. Lee*. New York: Alfred Knopf, 1988.

Arnold, James. *Grant Wins the War: Decision at Vicksburg*. New York: John Wiley and Sons, 1997.

Bailey, Ronald. *Forward to Richmond: McClellan's Peninsular Campaign*. Alexandria, Va.: Time-Life Books, 1983.

Ballard, Michael. *Civil War Mississippi: A Guide*. Jackson: University Press of Mississippi, 2000.

———. *Pemberton: A Biography*. Jackson: University Press of Mississippi, 1991.

———. *Vicksburg*. Chapel Hill: University of North Carolina Press, 2004.

Bartlett, John. *Bartlett's Familiar Quotations*. 15th ed. Boston: Little, Brown, 1980.

Basler, Roy, ed. *The Collected Works of Abraham Lincoln*. Vol. 4. New Brunswick, N.J.: Rutgers University Press, 1953.

Bauer, K. Jack. *The Mexican War: 1846–1848*. New York: Macmillan, 1974.

Bearss, Edwin Cole. *Campaign for Vicksburg*. 3 vols. Dayton, Ohio: Morningside House, 1986.

Beauregard, Pierre G. T. "The First Battle of Bull Run." In *Battles and Leaders of the Civil War*, 1:196–227. Edison, N.J.: Castle, 1995.

Beringer, Richard, Herman Hattaway, Archer Jones, and William Still. *Why the South Lost*. Athens: University of Georgia Press, 1986.

Bill, Alfred. *Rehearsal for Conflict: The War with Mexico, 1846–1848*. New York: Cooper Square, 1969.

Blakey, Arch Fredric. *General John H. Winder, C.S.A.* Gainesville: University of Florida Press, 1990.

Boatner, Mark. *The Civil War Dictionary*. New York: David McKay, 1959.

Canfield, Cass. *The Iron Will of Jefferson Davis*. New York: Fairfax Press, 1978.

Carney, Stephen. *Gateway South: The Campaign for Monterey*. Washington, D.C.: Center of Military History, U.S. Army, 2005.

———. *Guns along the Rio Grande: Palo Alto and Resaca de la Palma.* Washington, D.C.: Center of Military History, U.S. Army, 2005.

Catton, Bruce. *The Army of the Potomac: Glory Road.* Garden City, N.Y.: Doubleday, 1952.

———. *Army of the Potomac: Mr. Lincoln's Army.* Garden City, N.Y.: Doubleday, 1962.

———. *The Civil War.* New York: American Heritage Press, 1960.

———. *This Hallowed Ground.* Garden City, N.Y.: Doubleday, 1956.

Chaitin, Peter. *The Coastal War: Chesapeake Bay to Rio Grande.* Alexandria, Va.: Time-Life Books, 1984.

Chandler, David. *The Campaigns of Napoleon.* New York: MacMillan, 1966.

Clancey, Tom. *Into the Storm: A Study in Command.* New York: G. P. Putnam's Sons, 1997.

Clausewitz, Carl von. *On War.* Ed. Michael Howard and Peter Paret. Princeton, N.J.: Princeton University Press, 1976.

Cleaves, Freeman. *Meade of Gettysburg.* Norman: University of Oklahoma Press, 1960.

———. *Rock of Chickamauga: The Life of General George H. Thomas.* Westport, Conn.: Greenwood, 1974.

Conn, Stephen. *American Military History.* Washington, D.C.: Center of Military History, U.S. Army, 1989.

Cullum, George W. *Biographical Register of the Officers and Graduates of the United States Military Academy.* Vol. 1. Boston: Houghton Mifflin, 1891.

Daniel, Larry. *Shiloh.* New York: Simon and Schuster, 1997.

Davis, Burke. *Gray Fox.* New York: Rinehart, 1956.

Donald, David, ed. *Why the North Won the Civil War.* New York: Collier Books, 1962.

Donovan, Timothy, et al. *The American Civil War.* West Point, N.Y.: U.S. Military Academy, 1980.

Dougherty, Kevin. "The Use of Artillery during MOUT." *Army Trainer* (Summer 1991): 16–17.

Doughty, Robert. *American Military History and the Evolution of Warfare in the Western World.* Lexington, Mass.: D. C. Heath, 1996.

Dowdey, Clifford. *The Land They Fought For.* Garden City, N.Y.: Doubleday, 1955.

———. *The Seven Days.* New York: Fairfax Press, 1978.

Dowdey, Clifford, and Louis Manarin, eds. *The Wartime Papers of R. E. Lee.* New York: Bramhall House, 1961.

Dufour, Charles. *The Mexican War: A Compact History, 1846–1848.* New York: Hawthorne Books, 1968.

Echoes of Glory: Arms and Equipment of the Union. Alexandria, Va.: Time-Life Books, 1998.

Eckenrode, H. J., and Bryan Conrad. *James Longstreet: Lee's War Horse.* Chapel Hill: University of North Carolina Press, 1986.

Eisenhower, Dwight. *Crusade in Europe.* Garden City, N.Y.: Doubleday, 1949.

Eisenhower, John S. D. *Agent of Destiny: The Life and Times of General Winfield Scott*. New York: Free Press, 1997.

———. *So Far from God: The U.S. War with Mexico, 1846–1848*. New York: Random House, 1989.

Eldredge, Z. S. *The Beginnings of San Francisco from the Expedition of Anza, 1774 to the City Charter of April 15, 1850, with Biographical and Other Notes*. San Francisco: Z. S. Eldredge, 1912, http://www.webroots.org/library/usahist/tbosfooo.html (accessed March 8, 2005).

Faulkner, William. *Intruder in the Dust*. New York: Random House, 1948.

Feis, William. *Grant's Secret Service*. Lincoln: University of Nebraska Press, 2002.

Flood, Charles Bracelen. *Grant and Sherman: The Friendship that Won the Civil War*. New York: Farrar, Straus and Giroux, 2005.

FM 3-0. *Operations*. Washington, D.C.: Headquarters, Department of the Army, 2001.

FM 22-100. *Army Leadership*. Washington, D.C.: Headquarters, Department of the Army, 1999.

Fonvielle, Chris. *The Wilmington Campaign*. Mechanicsburg, Pa.: Stackpole, 2001.

Foote, Shelby. *The Civil War: A Narrative*. Vol. 2. New York: Random House, 1963.

Freeman, Douglas Southall. *Lee's Lieutenants: A Study in Command*. 3 vols. New York: Charles Scribner's Sons, 1942–1944.

———. *R. E. Lee: A Biography*. 4 vols. New York: Charles Scribner's Sons, 1934.

Fried, Joseph. "Murder of a Union General." *Civil War Times Illustrated* 1 (June 1962): 14-16.

Gabel, Chris. *Railroad Generalship: Foundations of Civil War Strategy*. Fort Leavenworth, Kans.: Combat Studies Institute, 1997.

———. *Staff Ride Handbook for the Vicksburg Campaign December 1862–July 1863*. Fort Leavenworth, Kans.: U.S. Army Command and General Staff College, 2001.

Glatthaar, Joseph. *Partners in Command: The Relationship between Leaders in the Civil War*. New York: Free Press, 1994.

Goolrick, William. *Rebels Resurgent: Fredericksburg to Chancellorsville*. Alexandria, Va.: Time-Life Books, 1985.

Gordon, Leslie. *General George E. Pickett in Life and Legend*. Chapel Hill: University of North Carolina Press, 1998.

Grant, Ulysses. *Personal Memoirs of U. S. Grant*. Ed. E. B. Long. Reprint, New York: Da Capo Press, 1982.

Hallock, Judith. *Braxton Bragg and Confederate Defeat*. Vol. 2. Tuscaloosa: University of Alabama Press, 1991.

Harris, Shawn. "Lion's Tail Touched." *Military History* (June 1998): 42–48.

Hart, B. H. Liddell. *Sherman: Soldier, Realist, American*. Westport, Conn.: Greenwood Press, 1978.

Hassler, William. *A. P. Hill: Lee's Forgotten General*. Richmond, Va.: Garrett and Massie, 1957.

Hattaway, Herman, and Archer Jones. *How the North Won.* Urbana: University of Illinois Press, 1983.

Hebert, Walter. *Fighting Joe Hooker.* Lincoln: University of Nebraska Press, 1999.

Henderson, G. F. R. *Stonewall Jackson and the American Civil War.* 2 vols. New York: Smithmark, 1994.

Henry, Robert Selph. *Nathan Bedford Forrest: First with the Most.* New York: Smithmark, 1994.

———. *The Story of the Mexican War.* New York: Frederick Ungar, 1950.

Hill, Daniel H. "Chickamauga—The Great Battle of the West." In *Battles and Leaders of the Civil War,* 3:638–662. Edison, N.J.: Castle Books, 1995.

———. "McClellan's Change of Base and Malvern Hill." In *Battles and Leaders of the Civil War,* 2:383–395. Edison, N.J.: Castle Books, 1995.

Hughes, Nathaniel, and Gordon Whitney. *Jefferson Davis in Blue: The Life of Sherman's Relentless Warrior.* Baton Rouge: Louisiana State University Press, 2002.

Hunt, Henry. "The First Day at Gettysburg." In *Battles and Leaders of the Civil War,* 3:255–284. Edison, N.J.: Castle Books, 1995.

Johnston, Joseph. *Narrative of Military Operations Directed during the Late War between the States.* 1874. Reprint, Bloomington: Indiana University Press, 1959.

Jones, Archer. *Civil War Command and Strategy.* New York: Free Press, 1992.

Krick, Robert. "Sleepless in the Saddle: Stonewall Jackson in the Seven Days." In *The Richmond Campaign of 1862,* ed. Gary Gallagher, 66–95. Chapel Hill: University of North Carolina Press, 2002.

Kuehl, Daniel. "Double-shot Your Guns and Give 'em Hell!: Braxton Bragg and the War in Mexico." *Civil War History* 38, no. 1 (March 1991): 50–65.

Lawrence, Dan. *Company A, 2nd U.S. Artillery History.* http://www.cottonbalers.lynchburg.net/artillery.htm (accessed September 25, 2004).

Lewis, Lloyd. *Sherman: Fighting Prophet.* New York: Harcourt, Brace, 1932.

Longstreet, James. *From Manassas to Appomattox.* Secaucus, N.J.: Blue and Grey Press, 1984.

Luvaas, Jay. "Kennesaw Mountain." In *The Civil War Battlefield Guide,* ed. Frances Kennedy, 187–191. Boston: Houghton Mifflin, 1990.

Manchester, William. *American Caesar: Douglas MacArthur, 1880–1964.* Boston: Little, Brown, 1978.

Marszalek, John. *Sherman: A Soldier's Passion for Order.* New York: Free Press, 1993.

Matloff, Maurice. *American Military History.* Washington, D.C.: Office of the Chief of Military History, U.S. Army, 1969.

Maurice, Frederick. *Robert E. Lee: The Soldier.* New York: Bonanza Books, 1925.

McClellan, George. "The Penisular Campaign." In *Battles and Leaders of the Civil War,* 2:160–187. Edison, N.J.: Castle, 1995.

McDonough, James. *Shiloh: In Hell before Night.* Knoxville: University of Tennessee Press, 1977.

McFeely, William. *Grant: A Biography*. New York: W. W. Norton, 1982.

McWhiney, Grady. *Braxton Bragg and Confederate Defeat*. Vol. 1. New York: Columbia University Press, 1969.

———. "Jefferson Davis and the Art of War." *Civil War History* 22, no. 11 (June 1975): 101–112.

McWhiney, Grady, and Perry Jamieson. *Attack and Die: Civil War Military Tactics and the Southern Heritage*. University: University of Alabama Press, 1982.

Millett, Allan, and Peter Maslowski. *For the Common Defense: A Military History of the United States of America*. New York: Free Press, 1984.

Mills, Walter. *Arms and Men*. New York: G. P. Putnam's Sons, 1956.

Nevin, David. *The Road to Shiloh*. Alexandria, Va.: Time-Life Books, 1983.

Nevins, Allan. *The War for the Union*. Vol. 2. New York: Charles Scribner's Sons, 1960.

———. *The War for the Union*. Vol. 6. New York: Charles Scribner's Sons, 1960.

———. *The War for the Union*. Vol. 8. New York: Charles Scribner's Sons, 1971.

O'Connor, Richard. *Thomas: Rock of Chickamauga*. New York: Prentice-Hall, 1948.

Parish, Peter. *The American Civil War*. New York: Holmes and Meier, 1975.

Pemberton, John C. *Pemberton: Defender of Vicksburg*. Chapel Hill: University of North Carolina Press, 1942.

Peskin, Allan. *Winfield Scott and the Profession of Arms*. Kent, Ohio: Kent State University Press, 2003.

Piston, William. *Lee's Tarnished Lieutenant*. Athens: University of Georgia Press, 1987.

Pollard, E. A. *The Lost Cause*. New York: E. B. Treat, 1867.

Rafuse, Ethan. *McClellan's War*. Bloomington: Indiana University Press, 2005.

Randall, J. G. *The Civil War and Reconstruction*. Boston: D. C. Heath, 1937.

Robertson, James. *General A. P. Hill: The Story of a Confederate Warrior*. New York: Random House, 1987.

———. *Stonewall Jackson: The Man, the Soldier, the Legend*. New York: MacMillan, 1997.

Rosengarten, Theodore. *Tombee: Portrait of a Cotton Planter*. New York: William Morrow, 1986.

Schwarzkopf, Norman. *It Doesn't Take a Hero*. New York: Bantam Books, 1992.

Scott, Winfield. *Memoirs*. 2 vols. New York: Sheldon, 1864.

Sears, Louis Martin. *John Slidell*. Durham, N.C.: Duke University Press, 1925.

Sears, Stephen. *Chancellorsville*. Boston: Houghton Mifflin, 1996.

———. *George B. McClellan: The Young Napoleon*. New York: Ticknor and Fields, 1988.

———. *To the Gates of Richmond: The Peninsular Campaign*. New York: Ticknor and Fields, 1992.

Seitz, Don. *Braxton Bragg: General of the Confederacy*. Columbia, S.C.: State Company, 1924.

Shaara, Michael. *Killer Angels*. New York: Ballantine Books, 1975.

Sherman, William. *Memoirs of General William T. Sherman*. 2 vols. New York, 1875.

Simpson, Brooks, and Jean Berlin, eds. *Sherman's Civil War: Selected Correspondence of William T. Sherman, 1860–1865*. Chapel Hill: University of North Carolina Press, 1999.

Simpson, W. A. *The Second Regiment of Artillery*. http://www.army.mil/cmh-pg/books/R&H/R&H-2Art.htm (accessed September 30, 2004).

Smith, Jean Edward. *Grant*. New York: Simon and Schuster, 2001.

Smith, Stuart. *Douglas Southall Freeman on Leadership*. Shippensburg, Pa.: White Mane, 1993.

Stackpole, Edward. *They Met at Gettysburg*. Mechanicsburg, Pa.: Stackpole Books, 1956.

Stauffer, Alvin. "The Quartermaster's Department and the Mexican War." *Quartermaster Review* (May–June 1950): 1–6.

Stiles, T. J. *In Their Own Words: Civil War Commanders*. New York: Perigee, 1995.

Stokes, G. P. "Naked Sword in Hand." *Military History* (August 1991): 45–49.

Surdam, David. "The Union Navy's Blockade Reconsidered." *Naval War College Review* 51, no. 4 (Autumn 1998): 85–107.

Taylor, John. *General Maxwell Taylor: The Sword and the Pen*. New York: Doubleday, 1989.

Thomas, Emory. *The Confederate Nation*. New York: Harper and Row, 1979.

———. *Robert E. Lee*. New York: W. W. Norton, 1997.

Time-Life Editors. *Lee Takes Command*. Alexandria, Va.: Time-Life Books, 1984.

Traas, Adrian. *From the Golden Gate to Mexico City: The U.S. Army Topographical Engineers in the Mexican War, 1846–1848*. Washington, D.C.: Office of History, Corps of Engineers and Center of Military History, 1993.

Tucker, Glenn. *The Battle of Chickamauga*. New York: Eastern Acorn Press, 1981.

———. *Hancock the Superb*. Indianapolis: Bobbs-Merrill, 1960.

Vandiver, Frank. *Mighty Stonewall*. College Station: Texas A & M University Press, 1957.

Van Doren Stern, Philip. *The Confederate Navy: A Pictorial History*. Garden City, N.Y.: Doubleday, 1962.

Wallace, Edward. *General William Jenkins Worth: Monterey's Forgotten Hero*. Dallas: Southern Methodist University Press, 1953.

Warner, Ezra. *Generals in Blue*. Baton Rogue: Louisiana State University Press, 1964.

———. *Generals in Gray*. Baton Rogue: Louisiana State University Press, 1959.

Waugh, John. *Class of 1846*. New York: Warner Books, 1994.

Weddle, Kevin. "The Blockade Board of 1861 and Union Naval Strategy." Video. Carlisle Barracks, Pa.: U.S. Army War College, Department of Distance Education Library. Recorded June 16, 2004.

———. *Lincoln's Tragic Admiral: The Life of Samuel Francis Du Pont*. Charlottesville: University of Virginia Press, 2005.

Weigley, Russell. *The American Way of War*. Bloomington: University of Indiana Press, 1973.

———. *History of the United States Army*. New York: MacMillan, 1967.

Wert, Jeffry. *General James Longstreet: The Confederacy's Most Controversial Soldier—A Biography*. New York: Simon and Schuster, 1993.

Williams, Kenneth. *Lincoln Finds a General*. Vol. 1. New York: MacMillan, 1949.

Williams, T. Harry. *The History of American Wars*. New York: Alfred A. Knopf, 1981.

———. *Lincoln and His Generals*. New York: Alfred A. Knopf, 1952.

———. *P. G. T. Beauregard: Napoleon in Gray*. New York: Collier Books, 1962.

Willson, Beckles. *John Slidell and the Confederates in Paris (1862–65)*. New York: Minton, Balch, 1932.

Woodworth, Steven. *Jefferson Davis and His Generals: The Failure of Confederate Command in the West*. Lawrence: University Press of Kansas, 1990.

Young, John Russell. *Around the World with General Grant*. Ed. Michael Fellman. 1879. Reprint, Baltimore: Johns Hopkins University Press, 2002.

INDEX

Alexander, E. P., 32, 108

Anaconda Plan, 21, 66–68

Antietam, 145, 177

Armistead, Lewis, 12, 167, 168, 180–83, 184

Artillery, 10–12, 33, 39, 105–9, 135, 154–57, 162, 184, 185, 186

Atlanta Campaign, 24–25, 96

Aztec Club, 180–81

Banks, Nathaniel, 48, 97

Barksdale, William, 107–8

Barton, Clara, 27

Beauregard, Pierre Gustave Toutant (P. G. T.), 1, 29, 71, 97, 118, 122–26, 183

Benjamin, Judah, 60, 94, 139

Benton, Thomas Hart, 18–19

Bliss, William, 31

Blockade, 1, 56–63, 66, 146, 186

Bragg, Braxton, 8, 12, 97, 111–14, 126, 132, 133–37, 184

Breastworks (fortifications), 22, 23, 24–25, 34, 112, 160, 162–63

Buckner, Simon, 134, 152–53, 181

Buell, Don Carlos, 89

Buena Vista, 5, 13, 16, 23, 71, 72, 101, 110, 112, 114, 127–30, 131, 133, 135–36

Burnside, Ambrose, 14, 92, 107–8

Butler, Benjamin, 98

Butler, William, 18, 175

Butterfield, Daniel, 93

Cadwallader, George, 92

Camargo, 7, 26, 72, 74

Cavalry, 30, 34, 47–48, 52, 95, 121

Cedar Mountain, 176, 178

Censorship (freedom of the press), 20, 139, 140

Cerro Gordo, 29, 45, 101, 118–20, 121, 122, 185

Champion's Hill, 50

Chancellorsville, 82, 121–22, 160, 178, 185

Chapultepec, 5, 23, 92, 105, 109, 122, 134, 149–50, 155–56, 158–59, 164–66, 168, 180–81, 185, 186

Chattanooga, 8, 111–14, 134

Chickamauga, 8, 110, 112–14, 134

Churubusco, 29, 46, 51, 65, 158–59, 181

Clausewitz, Carl von, 20, 42

Cleburne, Patrick, 134

Command and control, 5–7, 33

Communications, 31–33, 55

Comstock, Cyrus, 107

Conciliation, 21, 78–79

Conscription (draft), 4, 16–17, 20

Contreras, 46, 51, 65, 150–51

Corinth, 102

Crimean War, 4, 26, 37, 60

Cullum, George, 101–2
Cushing, Caleb, 92

Davis, Jefferson (Confederate), 4, 9, 12,
    19–20, 37, 60, 97, 98, 101, 127–32, 133–
    37, 139, 146, 147, 151, 153, 185
Davis, Jefferson (Federal), 12, 86–90,
    184
Defensive, 1, 5, 11–12, 22–25, 33, 34, 51,
    126, 128, 155, 160–63, 171, 183
Depots (supply), 25, 47
Dix, Dorothea, 27
Duncan, James, 105–6, 185
Du Pont, Samuel, 1, 56–63, 184, 186

Elements of combat power, 1
Emancipation Proclamation, 21, 146–47
Engineers and engineering, 23–25, 28–29,
    31, 34, 37, 71, 117–19, 122
Envelopment, 6, 24, 52
Ewell, Richard, 52, 55, 98

Firepower, 9–12, 33
Floyd, John, 152–53
Foraging, 26, 47, 48–50, 73, 77
Forrest, Nathan Bedford, 48
Fort Donelson, 101–2
Fredericksburg, 24, 92, 107–9, 160,
    163, 178
Fremont, John, 20, 71, 97, 100–1
Frontal attack, 1, 6, 22, 24, 29, 33, 37,
    65, 121, 124–26, 163, 166, 170, 183,
    185, 186

Gaines's Mill, 160
Gettysburg, 13, 30, 81, 121–22, 160–61,
    166–68, 180, 182–83, 185
Grand Gulf, 48
Granger, Gordon, 114
Grant, Ulysses, 12, 13, 14, 18–19, 22, 25, 43,
    45–50, 52, 69–70, 80, 83, 96, 99, 103–

4, 110, 111, 124, 126, 147, 152–53, 169–72,
    183, 185
Grierson, Benjamin, 171–72

Halleck, Henry, 12, 15, 49, 71, 97, 100–4,
    147, 184
Hamer, Thomas, 31, 91–92
Hancock, Winfield Scott, 83, 180–83
Harney, William, 52
Hatteras Inlet, 60
Hill, A. P., 12, 54–55, 174–79, 184
Hill, D. H., 134
Hitchcock, Ethan Allen, 28, 31, 46
Holly Springs, 47
Hooker, Joseph, 12, 14, 29, 31, 53, 82, 91–
    95, 184, 185
Hunt, Henry, 85, 105–9, 184, 185

Infantry, 3–4, 108–9
Information, 28–33, 34
Intelligence, 28–30, 34, 93–95, 120–21,
    130, 139, 173
Interior lines, 2, 8, 50

Jackson (Mississippi), 50
Jackson, Thomas (Stonewall), 3, 14, 23,
    54, 80, 98, 109, 121, 154–57, 160, 161,
    175–78, 184, 186
Jessup, Thomas, 7
Johnston, Albert Sydney, 123–24
Johnston, Joseph, 23, 24–25, 29, 39–40,
    48, 50, 71, 121, 137, 171
Jomini, Antoine Henri, 2, 14, 33

Kearney, Philip, 12, 51–55, 184
Kearney, Stephen, 20
Kennesaw Mountain, 24–25
Keyes, Erasmus, 39–40

Lane, James, 86–87
Lane, Joseph, 86–87

Leadership, 12–22, 33–34, 70, 80, 133–34, 170, 185

Lee, Robert E., 1, 12, 13, 14, 28, 29, 30, 31, 40, 50, 54, 60, 71, 80, 81, 82–84, 98, 117–21, 126, 131–32, 139, 146, 160–61, 167, 174, 175–78, 182, 183, 185

Letterman, Jonathan, 27

Limited war, 21, 33, 42, 64–68, 71, 79, 185, 186

Lincoln, Abraham, 14, 16, 17, 19–20, 21, 37, 42–44, 54, 58, 66, 79, 83–85, 96–97, 98, 102–4, 146, 147, 153

Little Round Top, 83

Logistics and supply, 22, 25–26, 33–34, 37, 45–50, 56–63, 65, 72, 110–11, 183, 185, 186

Longstreet, James, 8, 22, 53, 83, 112, 134, 158–63, 165–67, 175, 181, 182, 184

Magruder, John, 38–40, 154–56

Mahan, Dennis Hart, 15

Malvern Hill, 54, 79

Manassas, 8, 13, 17, 27, 54, 66, 96, 123, 177

Maneuver, 1–8, 33, 40, 45, 50, 62, 65, 68, 172

McClellan, George, 1, 4, 13, 14, 16, 19, 20, 21, 28, 29, 31, 37–44, 52–54, 66, 71, 79–80, 93, 101, 102, 104, 106, 146, 184, 185, 186

McClernand, John, 48, 98

McDowell, Irvin, 13, 14, 96, 98, 123

Meade, George, 7, 12, 14, 16, 70, 71, 80, 81–85, 126, 161

Medical services, 26–28, 34

Mexico City, 3, 13, 18, 21, 25, 28, 46, 51, 52, 55, 64–65, 68, 92, 134, 146, 155, 164–65, 170, 181

Minié ball, 3, 9–10, 28, 33

Mississippi Rifles, 9, 127–28

Molino del Ray, 105, 158, 159, 170, 181

Monterey, 13, 32, 71, 81–82, 83, 85, 110, 114, 158

Munford, Tom, 156–57

Murfreesboro, 110, 111

Napoleon and Napoleonic tactics, 2, 4, 11–12, 15, 25, 33, 68, 105, 155, 156

Nashville, 110, 186

Navy Board, 58–59

Nelson, William, 87–90

Objective, as a principle of war, 20–22, 42, 44

Offensive, 11, 22, 23–24, 34, 40, 121, 126, 158–63, 166, 172, 184, 186

Ord, E. O. C., 97

Palo Alto, 11, 105, 108, 158

Patterson, Robert, 18, 41, 98

Pedregal, 29

Pemberton, John, 12, 22, 28, 47, 50, 169–73, 184, 185

Peninsula Campaign, 13, 14, 29, 37, 38–42, 52–54, 79, 146, 160, 175

Peter Principle, 98, 173

Pickett, George, and Pickett's Charge, 1, 5, 83, 159, 164–68, 181, 184, 185

Pierce, Franklin, 127, 151

Pillow, Gideon, 12, 19–20, 41, 92, 147–53, 155–56, 175, 179, 185

Pinkerton, Allan, 93–94

Poinsett, Joel, 10, 105

Political generals and political considerations, 17–20, 41–43, 92, 98, 147–53

Polk, James, 16, 17–19, 20–21, 32, 37, 41–43, 64, 82, 84, 92, 97, 146, 148, 150–51, 153

Polk, Leonidas, 112, 134

Pope, John, 12, 14, 54, 69–80, 81, 176, 185; general orders, 73–78, 80

Port Royal Sound, 59–62

Prentiss, Benjamin, 125
Protection, 22–28, 34
Puebla, 13, 46

Railroad, 7–8, 33, 47–48, 74–75, 111
Reconnaissance, 28, 29, 53, 69, 117–21,
    130, 185
Resaca de la Palma, 13, 105, 158, 169
Reynolds, John, 16, 83, 126
Reynosa, 72, 86
Richmond, 138–42
Rifle, and the associated impact on tac-
    tics, 3–4, 9–10, 11–12, 22, 24, 33, 154,
    162–63
Rosecrans, William, 111–12, 114

Sanitation Commission, 26
Santa Anna, Antonio Lopez de, 3, 23, 30,
    51, 68, 101, 120–21, 128–29
Scott, Winfield, 3–4, 5, 9, 11, 13, 14–15,
    17–19, 21, 22, 25, 28, 29, 30–31, 37, 41–
    44, 45–50, 52, 64–68, 69–73, 80, 92,
    97, 101, 104, 110, 117–20, 121, 122–23,
    126, 130, 148, 149–51, 155, 164–65, 170,
    185, 186
Sevastopol, 38, 39, 40, 60
Seven Days Battles, 91
Seward, William, 42–43
Sharpe, George, 29, 93–94
Shenandoah Valley, 3, 8, 74, 157
Sherman, William, 22, 24–25, 49–50, 96–
    99, 100, 101, 104, 184; march to the sea,
    50, 96
Shiloh, 13, 123–26
Siege, 37–41, 44, 50, 186
Slidell, John, 28, 143–46, 184
Sloat, John, 56
Smith, John, 29, 31, 121
Smith, Persifor, 91
Span of control, 12–13, 55

Staff, 15, 30–31, 34, 69–70, 82, 91–93, 95,
    101, 103, 130, 185
Steam power, 59–62
Stockton, Robert, 56
Stringham, Silas, 60
Stuart, Jeb, 30, 121, 177
Sumner, Edwin, 53

Tattnal, Joseph, 60–61
Taylor, Zachary, 5, 7, 13, 14, 16, 17–19, 20,
    23, 26, 30, 31, 32, 69–73, 78, 80, 81–83,
    85, 101, 104, 105, 110–11, 126, 127–30,
    134, 135–36, 146, 148, 169, 185
Telegraph, 32, 34, 74–75
Thayer, Sylvanus, 14–15, 23
Thomas, George, 12, 22, 110–14, 126,
    183, 185
Total war, 21, 22, 33
Tower, Zealous, 29, 121
Transportation, 7–8, 33, 47
Turning movement, 1, 5, 13, 29, 33, 37,
    69, 101, 120–21, 122–23, 125–26, 183,
    185
Twiggs, David, 13, 119, 149

Van Dorn, Earl, 47
Vera Cruz, 13, 18, 28, 30, 37–38, 40, 41, 42,
    44, 45, 47, 64, 68, 69, 70, 92, 101, 134,
    138–39, 142, 146, 186
Vicksburg Campaign, 22, 25, 45, 83, 169–
    73, 185
Volunteers, 3, 9, 15–17, 26, 34, 67–68, 71–
    73, 127, 132, 134

Wagons (supply), 25, 48–49
Warren, Gouverneur, 85
Welles, Gideon, 42
Wellington, Duke of, 25, 46–47, 129
West Point and West Pointers, 13, 14–15,
    23, 33, 68, 97, 127, 130

White Oak Swamp, 156–57
Wilderness, 12, 13
Williamsburg, 39, 53, 160, 175
Winder, John, 12, 138–42, 184, 186
Wool, John, 13, 18, 72–73, 128

Worth, William, 13, 47, 81, 106, 155, 165–66, 169–71, 174, 179, 185
Wright, Horatio, 88–89

Yorktown, 37, 38, 40, 41, 44, 53